ECONOMIC
PARABLES

ECONOMIC PARABLES

The Monetary Teachings of Jesus Christ

DAVID COWAN

Paternoster:
thinking faith

COLORADO SPRINGS · LONDON · HYDERABAD

Paternoster Publishing
A Ministry of Biblica
We welcome your questions and comments.

USA   1820 Jet Stream Drive, Colorado Springs, CO 80921 www.authenticbooks.com
UK   9 Holdom Avenue, Bletchley, Milton Keynes, Bucks, MK1 1QR
      www.authenticmedia.co.uk
India   Logos Bhavan, Medchal Road, Jeedimetla Village, Secunderabad 500 055, A.P.

Economic Parables
ISBN-13: 978-1-932805-72-7

Cover design: Paul Lewis
Interior design: Angela Lewis
Editorial team: Andy Sloan, Betsy Weinrich, Dana Bromley

Printed in the United States of America

≈ Contents ≈

This book is dedicated to

Hanny.

That's just the way it is!

PREFACE TO THE
SECOND EDITION

A second edition gives the author the opportunity to reflect on the intervening period since completing the first manuscript and the time when it has come close to the satisfaction of selling out of the first edition. This is great for the author. However, few books find their way into the eye of the storm, giving the author an opportunity to reflect on a major global event related to their book. Economic Parables is one of those rare books.

The global crisis should not have been a surprise. On page 79, I wrote: The fragility of debt is a big picture and small picture thing. The big picture is that we may be living in an economic bubble, and history teaches us that all economic bubbles burst. If this happens, many of us will be in deep trouble. The small picture is that people also experience their own personal bubble.

The bubble has now burst, and I have chosen to reflect a little bit on that in an afterword, in order to continue the debate I set out to tackle. I do, however, want to address here certain things that kept coming up in the many discussions I had with people since the book first appeared.

First, I do not advocate capitalism as a perfect system; merely that it offers us the most effective tools for the economic job at hand, and hence as Christians we have to engage with it. There is an assumption amongst critics that what we have is unregulated capitalism. We do not, and I don't believe even the staunchest supporters of capitalism advocate this. What we have in America and other leading economies is regulated capitalism, as Milton Friedman argued government has a role to ensure fair play by the rules. What has happened in recent times is that the rules, regulations, and common sense have all been breached. The banks got into a hole because they dug it themselves by breaking good banking sense. More about this is discussed in the afterword.

Second, I have not offered the answers at the back of the book. As individuals and communities, we have to figure out the common economic ground for discussing our faith in the economic world in which we find ourselves, using the words of Jesus. Too often theological ideas and political ideas are entwined, and I wish to separate them out in the book. The questions ending each chapter are critical to using this book, as they challenge assumptions I have made and prepare the reader to engage in a debate about how they understand the economy and how they can engage with it faithfully.

In a quick word of thanks, I would like to thank all those people who have bought and used the book to further their engagement with the economy, and all the radio talk show hosts who have graciously invited me on to their program to discuss the book and the economy. I would also like to thank the folks at B&B Media, publicists for the book, Audra Jennings, Tracy McCarter, and Jennifer Glenn. They have done an amazing job! Also, thanks again to Volney, Dana and Jourdan, and to Mike Dworak, for their belief in the book. A final word of thanks again to Hanny, David, and Yasmin for their love and support.

PREFACE TO THE FIRST EDITION

Books are written for many reasons and have various sources of development. This book is the result of over twenty years of reflection on economic issues from a theological perspective. I studied theology right after high school, then returned to university to reflect on the intervening period that was spent working in the finance industry, first as a journalist and then as a bank executive at an international clearing bank and at the World Bank Group in Washington DC.

My hope is that this book will spark debate within Christian churches and groups as to what is demanded of us in the globalized economic world in which we are called to serve as Christians. I have tried to be provocative, so that readers will be stimulated to discuss these issues with others and lead us into new conversations to change people's hearts as economic persons.

Each chapter sets out to discuss one of Jesus' parables in a strident way, and the questions at the end of the chapters focus on the points I raise and with which you may or may not agree. If I start a few lively debates, then I will have achieved what I attempted to do. If this conversation permeates the churches, then the book will have served an even more important purpose.

I would like to thank some people who have brought this book into being, since no book can be completed without many debts being owed to others for their support and efforts. At Paternoster and Authentic Media, first thanks should go to Robin Parry and Volney James for believing in the idea at the outset. Once in progress, Andy Sloan was a gift as an editor. I responded to his gentle chastising to get things done. Thanks also go to Angela Lewis, who has shepherded the book to completion.

I am grateful for the many people who have listened to my thoughts and given me the opportunity to express them in different settings. My thanks go especially to the chaplains at Oxford University (Somerville, St. Hugh's, St. John's, and the University Church of St. Mary's) and Cambridge University (Jesus, King's, St. Catherine's, Sydney Sussex), where I was able to set out my thoughts in the unique context of Evensong services, followed by many an interesting debate. My thanks also go to the Center for the Study of Religion at Princeton University, the Henry Martyn Centre at Westminster College in Cambridge, and my own college in Oxford, Regent's Park College, where some of the thoughts expressed in these pages were presented in seminars and lectures. Regent's provided me with an intellectual home in Oxford, and I am grateful to the Fellows there for instructing me, especially to Paul Fiddes and Tim Bradshaw for their continued support and friendship.

Thanks also go to the Evangelical Lutheran Church of England (ELCE) and Westfield House, the ELCE House of Studies, and in particular to Reg Quirk, who has listened to me with a patient ear these past years. My thanks to the congregations I have served and visited and with whom I shared many of the thoughts found herein, especially Resurrection in Cambridge, where the idea first took root. And to Graham Tomlin, my supervisor at Oxford and a great source of encouragement, now achieving great things as Principal of the St. Paul's Theological Centre at Holy Trinity Brompton in London.

On a personal level, my thanks go to Richard and to Daniel, to whom I offer this book in thanks.

Finally, to my wife Hanny, whose love and support these many years I would have been much the poorer without: I thank her for taking a journey with me with little idea of destination. Along our life's path together, we have been joined by David and Yasmin, who are just too wonderful for words.

David Cowan
Cluny, France
December 2006

CHAPTER 1

TO HIS DISCIPLES HE
EXPLAINED EVERYTHING

―――――――――――――― ⌒ ――――――――――――――

"With many similar parables Jesus spoke the word to them, as much as they could understand. He did not say anything to them without using a parable. But when he was alone with his own disciples, he explained everything."

—MARK 4:33–34

"The main thing about money, Bud, is that it makes you do things you don't want to do."

—HAL HOLBROOK'S CHARACTER, LOU MANNHEIM,

IN THE FILM *WALL STREET*

Have you ever wondered how you're going to pay the next bill? Worried about a job promotion? Felt the world is unfair in economic rewards? Envied a neighbor or a celebrity who seems to have it all? Been indecisive about how to invest your savings wisely? Been moved by the desperate poverty in your nation's cities or in poorer countries?

These are all economic questions, everyday examples of things that concern people around the world. If you have had such thoughts and wondered what your work and economic life as a Christian means, then this book is for you. It won't provide you with all the answers, but reading the reflections that make up this book will enable you to think more deeply on economic issues from a faith perspective.

Now you could just figure that the simple answer is to give everything up, walk out the door, and follow Jesus—as in the troubling story in the Bible about the young man who asks Jesus what he must do to achieve salvation, and Jesus tells him to go and sell all his possessions, give the money to the poor, and then come and follow Jesus. This is quite different from how Jesus called the Twelve. To them, he just said, "Follow me!"

What was Jesus playing at, testing this fellow to give up everything? The young man tells Jesus that he has kept all the commandments and asks what he still lacks. In Matthew 19:21, we read that Jesus said to him: "If you want to be perfect, go, sell your possessions and give to the poor, and you will have treasure in heaven. Then come, follow me." The young man finds this very difficult, so he disappears once more into the crowd.

At first glance, the answer the young man gets from Jesus seems to be an unworldly demand. How can he give up all he has and simply follow?

This story is often cited as the ultimate response to economics—a Christian ideal. Yet we wonder what would happen if Jesus were speaking to us today in our complex economic world. How can we give up all we have and simply follow? To answer this question we have to understand what Jesus was really saying to the young man, as well as the application of that message to our own lives. The general point Jesus is making is that wealth stands between people and discipleship. The particular point for this young man was for him to give up all he had—not just wealth, but family and friends—and simply follow Jesus to become a disciple.

When the young man asks, "What good thing must I do to get eternal life?" he crystallizes the paradox of material life. He asks the wrong question, for he is confronted by Jesus, who is the way of salvation. In asking the wrong question he is also answering it, drawing from Jesus the response to give up all he has and to follow him. Because his wealth and materialistic view of life blind him from seeing who Jesus truly is, the impossibility of the demand is immediately apparent to him. Faced with this, the young man disappears back into the crowd.

How often do *we* disappear into the crowd? Is it simplistic to think that Jesus, speaking to us today through this story, wants us to give up all we have? We know Jesus commands us to follow him, but what this means for us will vary according to our specific situation. Today, the economic world is complex. This does not excuse us from what true discipleship means, nor does it mean we lose sight of the simple command to follow Jesus. In many ways, our problems—facing debts or striving to provide for our children—are the same worries of the first followers. Jesus approached the first hearers of his word with many parables about such worries: concerns about work, debts, and daily needs. He used these stories to reveal the kingdom of heaven and his promises for those who choose to follow him.

Jesus used everyday examples in his parables because this met with his listeners' experience. A number of "economic parables" have been collected in this book. Some would contend that these parables are just allegories. But I believe we will discover that these parables have much to reveal to us in a world dominated by free enterprise and globalization.

As we begin to examine these economic parables, first we have to understand what parables are and why Jesus used them. We need to start by looking closely at the images and words Jesus used in order to understand what he was saying then and what he is saying to us today. Language today is often technical, and we are swamped with jargon and acronyms. Language can be used to exclude *or* include people. We can use jargon to draw people in or shut people out. When relating to people of other cultures and languages, we can speak our own language and make life even more difficult for them, or we can attempt to use their language to show compassion and respect.

For instance, the world of music has its own language, whether from the classical period of the symphony and opera or the popular music of hip-hop, house, garage, and other categories of sounds that are pumped out of our radios or iPods today. The church has its own language, replete with terms like *sin*, *grace*, and *forgiveness*. These terms mean something to those of us in the community of faith but are understood differently outside the church—and they are perhaps increasingly not properly understood at all.

The word *parable* is one of these words rooted in the community of faith. It is an Anglicized version of the New Testament Greek word *parabole*, which means the putting of one thing alongside another for comparison or illustration. The word is also linked to the Old Testament Hebrew word *mashal*, which has a number of illustrative uses. We usually think of a parable as an extended story or illustration, yet it can be as simple as a single sentence of wisdom, an ethical maxim, or a proverb. The word has other meanings in the Hebrew, such as an oracle or discourse or even a riddle. Jesus used many such expressions in his teaching, ranging from the proverb, "Physician, heal yourself!" to full-blown stories like most of the parables we will discover together in this book.

Jesus took an intriguing approach to using parables, as we learn in Mark 4:10–13:

> When he was alone, the Twelve and the others around him asked him about the parables. He told them, "The secret of the kingdom of God has been

given to you. But to those on the outside everything is said in parables so that, 'they may be ever seeing but never perceiving, and ever hearing but never understanding; otherwise they might turn and be forgiven!'"

Jesus employed everyday language and images in his parables to talk about God, the kingdom of God, and the life of faith. Jesus doesn't just use the term "the kingdom of God" and expect his hearers to understand right away. He says, "The kingdom of God is like . . ." and then adds the image of a farmer sowing seed, a pearl, a mustard seed, and other tangible objects or everyday images. In this way Jesus could get people's attention or make it easier for people to understand difficult things. The parables contained the grain of truth—"the word"—but the message was wrapped in a story of camouflage because the full impact was not intended for all hearers, as we see in Jesus' quotation of the prophet Isaiah in the passage in Mark 4. The full meaning was for those who had understood and were saved by "the word." The same remains true for us today because Scripture is "the Word of God."

There are, however, those who view Scripture as general moral advice rather than as an authority to live by, an authority that defines how the world really works. Yet we learn from Scripture how we are to understand faith as received by the grace of God. This goes beyond a general moral view, beyond advice about how to live a "good life" or create a "good society." When we live by faith, Scripture guides us in how to understand the world around us. The parables are given to us for illumination, and they are to be penetrated not by a general morality but by belief. The parables can be basically understood by anyone, so that the word they contain can take seed in the memory of the hearers and then eventually the truth can blossom in the hearts of those who truly hear. If this does not happen, then the judgment that they will not understand the parable will remain with them.

This means that it is only through true faith that the word is understood. Those who stand in unbelief never penetrate the word, so we should not be surprised when people give us a mystified look when we confess Christ, the one born of a virgin, the one resurrected and ascended, and all those points of doctrine that people find so hard to understand in our material world. This disbelief in our creed is not a new thing belonging to a secular age; it has always been so, as we see in Mark 4:33–34: "With many similar parables Jesus spoke the word to them, as much as they could understand. He did not say anything to them without using a parable. But when he was alone with his own disciples, he explained everything." If the seed of faith is within us and we have the word explained to us, then we will understand what the kingdom of God means for us and we will know what Jesus wants for us.

The trouble with Jesus is that he makes you do things you don't want to do! When he spoke to the young man, he knew what stood between the young man and discipleship. Jesus deliberately placed upon him what seems to be an impossible demand because his material things stood between him and God. In our modern economic world, we must ask ourselves the same question: What seemingly impossible demands does Jesus make on us?

By reading through these economic parables and listening directly to the words of Jesus, you can discover for yourself the answers to this question. This journey will surely enrich your faith; and some of the answers will be surprising, in part because Jesus was a more sophisticated economist than he is given credit for by the modern world. He understands the complexities of our world. He knows we can become enslaved to economic realities, but he also knows that we can live in this economic world in the light of the gospel. Many of the kinds of problems we have to face and the decisions we have to make have not changed in two thousand years. Jesus told stories using economic images and ideas because he understood that is how people in all times and places live. What is incredible is that Jesus can look at our complicated problems and address them in simple terms, such as a sower, a rich fool, or workers in a vineyard. All those listening to Jesus then knew what he was talking about, and we too can understand today.

The important point to make about our economy (or any economy, for that matter) is that our lives are to be lived in submission to God's will. When we look at life in this way, then his blessings follow. However, there has been a tendency among theologians to dismiss the modern economic world as ungodly. Capitalism, corporate enterprise, and the financial markets have been singled out for condemnation. The most overt attacks have come from the social gospel and liberation theology movements of the twentieth century. But there has been a propensity among many theologians to regard the economic arena as a place incompatible with faith. You will find a number of books written by theologians over the last hundred years attacking the capitalist economy in various parts of the world, particularly on the issue of poverty in urban America and in developing countries. These books favor a reading rooted in a material, socialist political understanding of economy rather than in Scripture. We saw this in the social gospel movement of the 1930s. Later we witnessed the birth of liberation, feminist, civil rights, human rights, and other movements that I contend likewise are driven more by secular theory than Scripture. The story of the young man and Jesus that we have looked at, and sayings like "Blessed are the poor" and "You cannot serve both God and Money," are taken as ruling out any commitment to working positively in our modern economy, since it is seen as a sphere beyond redemption.

To understand how we as Christians in the modern, globalized world can think about economic issues, we do need to understand the basis of the economic world. The bold claim I wish to make is that the common theological criticism is a result of a socialist understanding of the economy creeping into moral discourse. Socialism arose in Europe in reaction to the development of capitalism and eventually spawned communism and the Soviet Union. Socialism became cherished in the West as a moral political force—and communism as evidence of an alternative to capitalism. As long as communism existed, intellectuals in the West could argue that there was a valid alternative, even if it did not work very well. This gave them the confidence to imagine alternatives and inspired theologians to imagine that their moral critique could join forces with Christianity. For the most part, these theologians adopted a socialist critique as the "scientific" basis to their theological assault on capitalism, and more recently on globalization. The problem with socialism is that it is based on a view that humanity can improve and can strive, through its own will and power, to create a "good society." Scripture does not share this view because the purpose of life is reserved to God and because we are sinful individuals; therefore, our sinful nature will defeat any realization of such a society.

The fall of communism has left us with one economic system and that is capitalism in the form of the free market economy. Is capitalism bad? It has certainly been successful, lifting more people out of poverty than any plan advanced by socialists and other critics. In fact, socialism took people in the opposite direction, and you would be hard-pressed to name a single successful economy that is truly socialist. Many would argue that Europe has socialist economies, but in fact they are capitalist economies that are controlled by realistic socialists who abdicate their socialist theory to maintain their partisan grip on power.

The free enterprise system, for all its faults, works. This reality is important to reflect upon as we progress in our study because it is both a threat and an opportunity. The threat is to blindly bless the system; the opportunity is to utilize it as a tool (though imperfect) to help improve our communities. Capitalism promotes freedom and democracy since these are the conditions under which it works best. It has weaknesses because it is a way of organizing human beings, and therefore, like all things human, it is imperfect. The belief that the government can best direct the economy at the expense of private enterprise—and engineer a more moral society in the process—is ill-founded. Nevertheless, this belief appeals to advocates of a socialist basis to the economy because of the conviction that the state is more moral than the individual.

When it comes to the rules of science, Christians argue that God created the earth for humanity to harness and manage— and, therefore, potentially to abuse. Can we not say the same of the economy? In a large, interconnected world, couldn't it be that God has made the economic tools for the distribution of wealth, discovery of new foods, and extracting the goods of nature also open to abuse? This is not to say that economics is blessed, any more than we say that science is blessed. Both are tools for us to live in the world. If this argument holds, then we might say that the economy is theologically neutral, open to both good and bad uses.

You might ask at this point: Why should we care? Americans, in particular, generally approve of capitalism and perhaps do not perceive this to be a moral issue. There are intellectual influences in the United States that seek to undermine this positive view, however. And America is increasingly subject to economic change elsewhere in the world, such as the value of the dollar in international markets, cheaper labor, and demand for foreign products in the United States. American businesses sell to foreign markets and import from all over the world. They hire cheap labor from other countries rather than the more expensive American labor. The first anti-globalization riots occurred in Seattle, and various anti-globalization groups lobby in Washington, DC, and at World Bank meetings to get what they believe to be a better economic deal for the poor. Increasingly powerful environmental lobbyists have consistently attacked the Bush administration for defending American industrial interests by refusing to sign the Kyoto Protocol. Terrorism and Middle East politics have caused oil prices to rise, and environmental groups assail gas-guzzling American SUVs for threatening the planet. These are all examples of the global interconnectedness of the American economy; and we need to understand how we, as Christians, are supposed to live in this brave new world.

To help us in this quest, we need to recover the basics that Jesus taught and examine how we are to live out—within our economic system—those values. This does not mean that we need a "capitalist theology," but it does mean that we have to look at many reflections by theologians and statements made by church leaders with a fresh eye. We also need to ask whether we are like the young man Jesus confronts with his demand to follow. Many today would dismiss this as an unworldly demand. How can he give up all he has? How can we? The point is that this is not the real question. What the young man, and we today, ought to be asking is this: *Lord, because I am held hostage by all that I have and all that I am, what can I do?* We need to recognize that we are captive and that our freedom lies only in Christ—and that our aspiration should lie not in ambition but in communion with him. The young man was lost from the moment he asked the question because the way to salvation was staring him in the face. Jesus is the way, the truth, and the life; so instead of asking the question, he should have just followed.

All of us wonder how we can make a better life for ourselves and our family, how we can afford a new car or pay the kids' way through college. Yet how often do we ask ourselves how we are going to find salvation? In fact, we don't need to ask, because we simply turn to Jesus Christ and the question is answered at once. When we do that, then we will follow him. This book is about how we can follow Jesus in a complicated economic world by listening directly to his word in the parables he told.

Jesus sets out this simple command: "Follow me." These were the simple words he spoke to the Twelve. They listened, they obeyed, and they followed. Our discipleship also means hearing, obeying, and following Jesus. He will then guide us along the path of discipleship; he will tell us what our discipleship is to be about. For each of us the path is different: for some it may involve teaching or nursing, while for others it may mean being a business leader or a gas station attendant. Our work in the economy does not define our discipleship, but it is part of our vocation as Christians living and working in the world, influencing those around us for the better and taking the gospel to the four corners of the world. Whatever our calling, the Caller is the same. For the young man in the story, Jesus set an impossible command because he knew what stood between the young man and discipleship—namely, his love of wealth and material things. We can and should ask ourselves: *What stands between me and discipleship?*

Wealth and material things will not save us, nor will the pretense that we can build a good society. Though the economy we have is the most effective economy humanity has developed, we recognize that it is not possible to construct a perfect economy. The notion that we can save the world with just a little more cooperation and organization is a fallacy, for the world is fallen. Humanity *can* have an economic alternative that will make things better because economics is all about managing competing interests and forces. Humanity is in conflict, and the economy reflects this conflict. It is wrong to suggest that if we match progressive economic ideas with the gospel then we can have a divine economy. If we want to try to rule the economy with the gospel, then—to borrow from Martin Luther—we better fill the economy with real Christians first.

A key mechanism of the free market economy is self-interest. This was identified by Adam Smith, the Scottish moral philosopher, back in the eighteenth century. Smith did not think that self-interest merely means selfishness, however, because what is in our self-interest is not necessarily a selfish thing to do. There are many occasions in which we act selfishly, only to learn that we were not acting in our self-interest. You could take up gambling your hard-earned wages, but is it in your economic interest to gamble away your money and savings? What Jesus says is in our self-interest because, in the divine economy, it is salvation that is in our interest.

We cannot look at the problems of the world as something that can be solved simply by human ingenuity and economic manipulation. We have to look at what God intends—what his plan is for salvation in the world—since the ultimate solution is not of this world but of the kingdom that is to come. If we confuse our economic ideas with the gospel, then we are just offering secular salvation and competing in the supermarket of ideas. Jesus then becomes the brand logo contending with other great leaders of history and idealizations of the "good society" down through the ages. Remember this: In the divine economy, there is no competition. There is only one Lord. Let's listen to him.

Things to Think About

- Consider the young man who spoke to Jesus. What obstacle stands between you and God? What impossible demand might Jesus be making on you in this regard?

- What do you think Jesus meant when he referred to "treasure in heaven" in Matthew 19:21? How would you compare that treasure to the "treasures" you have now?

- Do you think people are basically greedy? Do corporations and business leaders promote greed? How about government, or even churches: Are they different than the commercial world?

- Try to imagine an alternative to today's economy. How would such a system operate? How does your understanding of human nature fit into this system?

- How do you suppose Jesus felt about the economy in his time? We will be exploring this throughout the book, but write down some reflections of "Jesus the economist"—and see if your conclusions are different by the end of our study.

CHAPTER 2

CAN WE USE WORLDLY WEALTH?

The Parable of the Dishonest Manager

LUKE 16:1–13

Introduction

This parable calls us to discern the difference between the negative force of greed and the positive force of faithful and honest self-interest. At the end of the parable, Jesus poses one of the most difficult economic points in the Bible: we cannot serve both God and wealth. Money is an inevitable reality of living in the world, and as such it can be used wisely—as long as it comes second to our relationship with God.

The Parable

Jesus told his disciples: "There was a rich man whose manager was accused of wasting his possessions. So he called him in and asked him, 'What is this I hear about you? Give an account of your management because you cannot be manager any longer.'

"The manager said to himself, 'What shall I do now? My master is taking away my job. I'm not strong enough to dig, and I'm ashamed to beg—I know what I'll do so that, when I lose my job here, people will welcome me into their houses.'

"So he called in each one of his master's debtors. He asked the first, 'How much do you owe my master?'

"'Eight hundred gallons of olive oil,' he replied.

"The manager told him, 'Take your bill, sit down quickly, and make it four hundred.'

"Then he asked the second, 'And how much do you owe?'

"'A thousand bushels of wheat,' he replied.

"He told him, 'Take your bill and make it eight hundred.'

"The master commended the dishonest manager because he had acted shrewdly. For the people of this world are more shrewd in dealing with their own kind than are the people of the light. I tell you, use worldly wealth to gain friends for yourselves, so that when it is gone, you will be welcomed into eternal dwellings.

"Whoever can be trusted with very little can also be trusted with much, and whoever is dishonest with very little will also be dishonest with much. So if you have not been trustworthy in handling worldly wealth, who will trust you with true riches? And if you have not been trustworthy with someone else's property, who will give you property of your own?

"No servant can serve two masters. Either he will hate the one and love the other, or he will be devoted to the one and despise the other. You cannot serve both God and Money."

The Reflection

The front-page headlines scream out at us: Corporate greed! Scandal! Enron! Worldcom! How comforting it must be for the media (and it can be for us, their readership) to be able to point to greed and say, "Aha! That's why it's wrong! It's big business!" Doing this, we place the blame somewhere else and let ourselves off the hook. In buying the newspaper, we purchase our peace of mind. In mouthing the condemnation, we seek absolution.

Yes, there is corporate greed, but greed is not exclusive to the world of business and finance. There is also greed in governments, charities, interest groups, churches, schools, and universities. There is greed anywhere there are people. It may be greed for career, for money, for power, for position, or for glory. It is all about us and what we want.

Ever since capitalism developed in the eighteenth century, it has had its critics. Today this criticism takes the form of anti-globalization activism, which is also the basis of intellectual criticism of capitalism. The protestors and intellectuals behave as if their identification and indictment of human greed is something new. But it isn't; it is ancient history. They are simply wrong. Greed is often confused with self-interest, which is the catalyst for the free market economy. Whether individuals, communities, governments, or businesses, we all act in our self-interest—and we need to understand what this reality means.

In Adam Smith's classic, eighteenth-century book on economics, *The Wealth of Nations*, he explained how self-interest is part of the central mechanism of the market economy. We'll say a little more about this in a later chapter, but in Smith's other significant work, *The Theory of Moral Sentiments*, we learn that self-interest does not necessarily equal greed. Self-interest is indeed an essential part of the market system, and wealth is generated through the free market. But greed is part of us; it is part of the fallen nature we struggle with as individuals. This parable in Luke 16 offers us a way to understand the negativity of greed and positive force of honesty, and the true relationship between self-interest and wealth.

The parable is given different names, such as the parable of the dishonest steward, the parable of the unjust steward, and the one I prefer—since it communicates more in today's terms— the parable of the dishonest manager. This is a difficult parable because we are to see the dishonest manager in a positive light. We are to admire him for his prudence, his astuteness, rather than for his commercial practices. In the commercial practice of the day, charging interest was forbidden. When the manager repackages the debts of his master's clients, there is little his master can do; for him to protest would be to declare that he himself had been dishonest. The master is caught in a conflict between two wrongs. Since this parable goes against the grain of our expectations, it is puzzling that Jesus tells it, isn't it?

This parable offers us a very worldly Jesus. He demands that the disciples use the tools and ways of the world in a worldly fashion. The worldly are wise by their own lights, acting prudently in their own interests. The sons and daughters of light are servants of God and often lack the wisdom to use their possessions in such a calculating way.

This is very much in contrast to the simple injunction of Jesus to give up all you have and follow. For here Jesus is saying to use "worldly wealth" (Luke 16:9) wisely. The fact that he says it is worldly lets us know that wealth can be acquired in unworthy ways. He goes further though, for wealth is neither a source of righteousness nor a means to salvation. It is simply a tool to be used. Paul wrote in 1 Timothy 6:10 that "the love of money is a root of all kinds of evil." Money itself is not "the root of all evil," although this verse is often misquoted to say just that. Jesus is saying that his followers must use wealth as a tool for spiritual purposes just as wisely as do the worldly.

Is this a case of the ends justifying the means? It is for those who use wealth purely for the sake of wealth because they only seek an earthly end. But it is not so in the case of the sons and daughters of light. Faithful disciples use their wealth, in fact all they have, in following Jesus. The question is *How are we to use our wealth?*—*and to what extent do we put material things before discipleship?*

We also have to ask what, in fact, it means to be "wealthy." I think it is safe to say that we are wealthy if we have the money to buy books like this, to go to school, to go on vacation, to watch cable television, to have mobile telephones, etc.—to have the things that citizenship in the West typically brings. Jesus said that a rich man finds it difficult to enter into heaven because in the comfort of such wealth it is all too easy to deny God and to revel in our own material life. This makes it harder for us to be disciples, for we can cast our glances elsewhere—away from God.

Of course, we can pretend that the "wealthy" are always other people: people like Bill Gates, Madonna, and Donald Trump. All too often our condemnation of wealth is a condemnation of others, for surely we are not wealthy in *that* way. Well, we are! We are wealthy because we live well; even when we are struggling we are better off than many others in the world.

Our earthly wealth is not ours. We only have stewardship of it from the creator of all things: God. Our goal as followers, as disciples, is the treasure that is in heaven. We are to use what we have in this life wisely. If we abuse wealth, then this *little* thing—which is little because ultimately wealth passes into dust—suggests that we are unfit for the *big* things, which are the treasures that await us in heaven after all that we are and have passes into dust. We are wrong to put our faith in our wealth, to allow wealth to become a barrier to genuine faith and discipleship. However, once we obey Christ's command to follow, then to neglect to use what we are given by God in good stewardship becomes a barrier to good discipleship.

This parable is followed by the simple statement that we cannot serve two masters: we must choose between God and Money (Luke 16:13). This is another saying that is often quoted as the decisive case against wealth. But Jesus doesn't use it that way. Jesus is warning us that by putting wealth first we become separated from God, and this will not do. Money is a tool of the world, and as such it can be used wisely, so long as it comes second to our relationship with God. God comes second when we are consumed by consumerism, choosing retail therapy over prayer. We choose a false god when we put our love of wealth before our love of God, when we put pursuit of material gain before discipleship. This is the real challenge for us, the great reversal that Jesus calls for in our lives.

We have economic tools; as sons and daughters of light, we are called to use them wisely, to be as prudent as those who are worldly by their own lights. We live in a world of the free market economy, and in recent decades big business and globalization have been regarded as tainted theologically. This is a criticism launched by theologians both in Europe and in America. The perception is one of threat: that we will be overwhelmed by forces beyond our control. Yet, we can picture this economy positively in the context of this parable. We can see that our wealth is a double-edged sword, capable of separating us from God *and* capable of helping us, our family, our community, the poor, and the world in general.

Wealth, or Money, in itself, is not the problem. The problem is how we use our wealth personally and in community. The assumption of critics is that the personal portion makes us greedy and the community portion is the best solution, the belief being that personal greed is overcome by a community spirit and by sharing. The individual is to be saved by the community—or, better still, the state. This has to be challenged. The flow needs to go the other way: where there are individuals who are more caring, there will be greater community. The other question we have to ask is if we really act differently with our wealth than with the other aspects of our lives. It is hard to believe that someone could be selfish in regard to money but not in regard to relating to others. The more selfish we are with our wealth, the more selfish we will be with our love for our spouse or in our attitude toward the needs of our neighbor.

Wealth is created by the sum of the actions of all participants: individuals, businesses, and government agencies. By working in the economy as responsible citizens, we are playing our part in generating wealth. In one sense we can feel bewildered by how small we are as individuals in this big, complex economy of ours. In another sense we can see how powerful individuals and groups of individuals can be. It doesn't take a village to innovate; some 95 percent of all new inventions in America are developed by entrepreneurs and small businesses. Some of these new inventions can make a huge impact on the lives of others. And this doesn't just mean iPods and other gadgets but innovations in areas like health care and communications, which can help improve the lives of those in the economy who are disadvantaged.

We have to be less selfish in all areas of our lives, reflecting on our lifestyles and checking ourselves against acting selfishly. We need to look at how selfishness translates into economic behavior, which is something we can change. If I change today, then maybe my neighbor will change tomorrow. There are many ways we can change our economic attitudes and actions. Here are a few possibilities to consider:

- *think* about the way we consume and what we consume

- *teach* our children to be wise consumers

- *realize* that what we consume has an impact on others

- *see* that much can be done by consumer power and word of mouth, persuading others to buy what is morally good and not buy what is morally bad for them

- *decide* carefully what to buy, not being impulsive or easily persuaded

- *give* more for God's work

- *invest* wisely for ourselves, our family, and our church community

In changing our actions we change our behavior as consumers in a way that can be calculated in the free enterprise system because the economy and businesses respond to changes in consumer behavior. Think back to all those TV reports on consumer spending leading up to Christmas, the downturn or upturn in retail confidence, and the "must have" toys. These aren't the tricks of stores trying to lure us into their portals; they are the statistical calculation of how we all behave as consumers.

There are many temptations in the marketplace because there is a demand for what is supplied—whether the virtue of that supply is positive or negative. For example, when the

Internet exploded onto the scene so did online pornography, unfortunately now one of the biggest online industries. And the Web's search engines, which are interesting measures of what people want to see, show that celebrities' names are regularly among the most frequent searches, confirming that our society is obsessed with star power. Thus our spending reveals a lot about us as individuals and about the community we live in. We can be thoughtful spenders or reckless spenders, and we can buy goods for wholesome, productive use or for our own self-destruction. The choice is ours.

Wealth can be either a barrier to discipleship or a healthy aspect of living out our discipleship. And wealth involves not only our money but also our time. When we are wealthy we have both more disposable income and greater potential for spending free time. That free time can be used in service. What is needed is energetic discipleship: a turning to Christ as the sole source of our being in the world, asking what he would have us do, how he would have us use "worldly wealth" wisely—if only we can say yes to his command to obey and follow.

Other Biblical Texts to Study

Luke 16:1   Luke 15:13, 30

Luke 16:8   Matthew 12:33; Luke 20:20–26

Luke 16:8   John 12:36; Ephesians 5:8;
                   1 Thessalonians 5:5

Luke 16:9   Matthew 19:21; Luke 11:41; 12:33

Luke 16:10–12   Matthew 25:19–23

Luke 16:13   Matthew 6:24

Things to Think About

- Why do you think the dishonest manager gets praised? Do you think that is right? What would you have done if you were his master?

- Do you think you are selfish? If so, in what ways? What steps can you take to be less selfish?

- Why do you think *money* is a negative word? How does Jesus give this negative word a positive use?

- Do you agree that wealth is a double-edged sword? What good things, and what bad things, could it do for you?

- Can you write down five ways in which you could change your attitude toward wealth, offering opportunities to use your wealth more wisely than you do now?

- How can you change your consumer behavior in general, and your spending in particular, for the better?

DO WE LET WEALTH
CHOKE THE WORD?

The Parable of the Sower

MATTHEW 13:18–23

Introduction

Do we let our wealth and work choke the Word of God? The setting of this parable was the rural economy of first-century Palestine, but it applies equally well to our complex modern economy. Jesus chose such rural images because they could be readily understood; he was not addressing the "environmental activists" of his day.

The Parable

"Listen then to what the parable of the sower means: When anyone hears the message about the kingdom and does not understand it, the evil one comes and snatches away what was sown in his heart. This is the seed sown along the path. The one who received the seed that fell on rocky places is the man who hears the word and at once receives it with joy. But since he has no root, he lasts only a short time. When trouble or persecution comes because of the word, he quickly falls away. The one who received the seed that fell among the thorns is the man who hears the word, but the worries of this life and the deceitfulness of wealth choke it, making it unfruitful. But the one who received the seed that fell on good soil is the man who hears the word and understands it. He produces a crop, yielding a hundred, sixty or thirty times what was sown."

The Reflection

We live in a noisy world. The television demands our attention, sirens thread their way through the night, and advertising screams out at us to buy the latest product or get a two-for-one deal. Everyone wants our attention! Little wonder that at times we feel information overload. So many words, so many images, so many sounds—all drowning our senses. It is easy to be like those in the parable of the sower who hear the word but are choked by "the worries of this life and the deceitfulness of wealth." In such a noisy world it is hard to hear the still, small voice of God's word in our midst.

Just before Jesus tells this parable, the disciples ask him why he speaks to the people in parables. Jesus tells them that it is hard for the people to know what the kingdom of God is like, so he uses images and ideas they are familiar with to then take them to the unfamiliar. He will speak to them in parables so they might hear the word; but they do not see, nor do they understand. This is the fulfillment of Isaiah's prophecy warning those who do not understand because their hearts are calloused and they hardly hear with their ears. It is difficult to hear the word in this noisy world of ours, and there is a danger that our hearts, too, become dull and we become heavy of hearing.

This parable has traditionally been interpreted as an allegory about the different kinds of hearers, those who are like stony soil and those who are like good soil. We can extend this to look at the soil we plant ourselves in, the setting in which we root our life and faith. And we might wonder if the global society in which we are planted is barren.

The economy of Jesus' time was much simpler than ours: a rural life of farming and cultivating fields and rocky places. The people listening to Jesus knew what he was talking about. Even those in the cities who were traders knew the ways and means of the rural economy. The hearers of the parable would have been familiar with the sower and his work. They understood how the seed was scattered and fell onto different types of soil and how the quality of the soil received the seed. They knew that the good soil would receive the seed and sustain it through the growing cycle, until the harvest.

For us as Westerners today, the sower is not a common sight on our landscape. Instead we have tractors and combine harvesters to take care of our harvest. The agricultural industry is overshadowed in many ways by the manufacturing and service industries. Nevertheless, it is still central to our modern economy and way of life. Together, all industries form the productive economy that feeds, shelters, clothes, and entertains us. In poorer countries, however, the means of farming is often little different from that described in the parable.

With the rise of environmentalism, we have seen the emergence of "eco-theologies." Whenever there is a shift in the secular world, this is matched by academic theology and church policy change. Environmentalism has been hitched to the wagon of stewardship. The new credo is *sustainability*, and anyone who doesn't fall into step is cast as reactionary or supporting evil. In the row over the Kyoto Protocol for carbon dioxide emissions, proposed as a way to battle global warming, the Bush administration and American industry have been painted as pariahs of environmental destruction.

Environmentalists see as foolish the idea that there is a legitimate alternative, based on economic arguments, to their view. The contention of the Bush administration is that the Kyoto treaty will damage American jobs. Free market economists argue that long-term change in technology will bring about improvement to the environment. After all, a hundred years ago people thought coal would run out, but new technology has improved efficiencies in the mining and use of coal—as well as produced alternative forms of energy. The environmental lobbyists appear to be suspiciously selective about knowledge, since there seems to be a bias against economics when deciding what has a good and bad impact. There is a romantic streak in environmentalism that "small is beautiful"; and so big business solutions are dismissed as driven by the ugly side of human nature in the pursuit of profit and greed.

According to this viewpoint big business is inherently damaging to God's creation and environmentalists have the moral high ground. However, we know that Jesus was not an eco-warrior, telling contemporary environmental fables. He was telling us that the word will fall on many places: business centers, shopping malls, universities, nightclubs, all places of our modern life. This is a story about where the word falls and where we have rooted our life. If our life is selfish, and all we want is to shop at the mall (or on eBay or Amazon) or be greedy for position, then we cannot be surprised if the word does not take root in such unfertile soil. The same is true for our community and nation. How can the word take root in a community that excludes God or a nation that does not stand under God?

In the economic realm, there are many places where the word needs to be heard. In our towns and cities on Sunday mornings, the bell is ringing up sales rather than calling people to worship. In halls of government and in company boardrooms, where difficult decisions affecting many are made, the word needs to be heard to guide those who make such decisions. In parks and back alleys, where the business of prostitution and exchange of drugs is rife, the word needs to be heard to snatch people off the streets and out of addiction. These are examples of the hard soil where people are rooted economically and in need of a way to find fertile soil in which they can grow.

Some argue that the inequalities of the capitalist system caused these problems in the first place. In this view, people are excluded and forced onto the margins of society. This economic view underpins social gospel thinking. However, this perspective is at odds with the world as it is and with the gospel as it is communicated in the Scriptures. The world as it is comprises people of conflicting wants, needs, and belief systems. The economy allows all people, regardless of their beliefs, to exchange. The gospel is offered to all, and the seed of the word falls where there is conflict and where people search for meaning.

The life of the Christian is guided by faith, and this comes before identifying with any other ideas. People can find themselves putting material things before their spiritual needs and commitment, which results in deeper spiritual emptiness. This can happen in different ways for different people. It happens when they put consumerism, a belief in salvation by secular means, or political ideology before God's demand on them. This can happen to Christians as well. They become consumers first, believers second. They seek secular salvation first, divine grace second. They tout their political identity first; their identification with Jesus comes second. These are all ways of looking at the world from the ground where the word must fall, but it is hard for the word to take root where fashion, humanism, or political zeal hardens the ground where the seed falls. These are ways of making the word conform to the needs and wishes of the one who spends, rallies, or postures rather than going on bended knee to receive God's grace.

Where the ground is fertile, the word takes root and drives out pride and anger and the sinful desires for baubles. If we respond to Jesus, then we can take our place in the community of redeemed sinners, showing the real presence of the word in the world. If we let the word take priority, then we will not become enslaved by a desire for wealth, we will not seek approval of others for our beliefs, and we will not raise our voice in violence. If we choose to root our life in Christ, then we are rooting our very being in the fertile soil that will allow us to blossom.

If we root our life in the path *next to* the fertile soil that Jesus sets out for us, then the word is not understood but is snatched away from us. This is like those who would place their faith in progressive ideas and want to build a perfect economic world. They seek to satisfy the desires of their selfish hearts rather than to have a heart that knows God. The rocky soil is for those who want to live a life of consumerism and self-indulgence, plucking pleasure from the passing moment. Among the thorns are people who know the price of everything but the value of nothing—those who will seek power for their own good and at the cost of their soul, ignoring the power of the truth that God offers freely.

To be in the good soil means understanding the original state of sin that prevents a progressive realization of society. It means knowing that merely seizing the passing moment is a denial of God's plan. It means not cynically manipulating position or wealth to get ahead in the world. To be in the good soil means asking in faith what we must do and being humbled by each faltering step we take in the world as we seek to answer God's call. This is the only way to live out the demands of the word. This is the only way to let the word take deep root and yield good fruit. This is not to say that we then become perfect, for all too often we still fall short of how God wants us to live. It does mean we know that when we fall he is there to offer us his hand and lead us toward doing better. When we try and fail, he is there to catch us. When we succeed, his Spirit and his word are present in us.

In this noisy world, where people shout for our attention or manipulate messages so that we might hear them, the word present in us shows its fruits. We don't need to shout or grab the headlines in order to demonstrate the work of the Lord. It is self-evident, it illuminates our understanding of the world, and it shines the light that others may see the word taking root. So many of the political and economic statements we hear from church leaders, such as their pronouncements that global trade is unjust and their constant calls for equal redistribution of wealth, seem to be "attention getters." The gospel then becomes one of many competing ideas, made to fit what people want to hear rather than what they need to hear. The Christian needs to be clear on the gospel, even when it sounds countercultural. Even in a wild garden, we may witness the beauty of a single flower that stands amidst the thorns.

Christians are a witness to God at work in the world, and we need the confidence to let his light shine in the world, rather than trying to be fashionable with our message. Certainly we can—indeed should—use the tools of modern communications to tell the story of Jesus and to let the world hear how salvation can be theirs. The tools of modern communications and globalization have opened many new possibilities for presenting the word to the world. We have the Internet, television, DVDs, and all manner of tools to be put to good use. The use of targeted communications can allow people in the most remote places to hear Christ's word. We are the sowers, not knowing exactly in what soil the word is being sown, but we can now scatter the seeds so much further. This should not be a triumph of style over substance, however, for the substance is contained in Scripture—it shines in the written words of Jesus. The means of spreading the word may change, but the message does not. Jesus tells us to expect people to reject him, to expect that many will not hear his word. We know the bottom line: that faith will not take root in those who settle in the wrong soil.

Other Biblical Texts to Study

Matthew 13:18	Mark 4:1–20; Luke 8:4–15
Matthew 13:19	Matthew 5:37
Matthew 13:21	Matthew 11:6
Matthew 13:22	Matthew 19:23; Romans 12:2; 1 Corinthians 1:20; 2:6, 8; 2 Corinthians 4:4; Galatians 1:4; 1 Timothy 6:9–10, 17
Matthew 13:23	John 15:1–8; Galatians 5:22–23; Philippians 1:9–11

Things to Think About

- Have you ever thought of your life in terms of the soil in which you are planted? How would you describe the soil in which your life is rooted right now?

- If the economy of this parable were to be applied to an urban setting, what images might you use?

- Do you agree or disagree that much of the economic debate offered by church leaders is about calling for just trade and equal redistribution of wealth? What should they say about the economy?

- Is it true to say the "social gospel" is a distortion? What approach do we need to address social issues today?

- Can we use this parable to understand and discuss environmental issues?

- Should churches advertise like Coca-Cola, Gap, or the latest blockbuster movie?

- What kind of an advertisement would you create for the gospel? For your church?

- Can faith grow in the wrong soil? Can faith grow in a state opposed to Christianity?

CHAPTER 4

DO WE ENVY OUR NEIGHBOR?

The Parable of the Workers in the Vineyard

MATTHEW 20:1–16

Introduction

Some of us are "doing better" than others. Some live in better neighborhoods, have better jobs, and earn more money. It seems that some people get better rewarded than others. Is this fair? Why should the economy not be prosperous for everyone? Of course, maybe we're just envious. The Bible tells us that God has provided for us all but challenges our generosity and pride.

The Parable

"For the kingdom of heaven is like a landowner who went out early in the morning to hire men to work in his vineyard. He agreed to pay them a denarius for the day and sent them into his vineyard.

"About the third hour he went out and saw others standing in the marketplace doing nothing. He told them, 'You also go and work in my vineyard, and I will pay you whatever is right.' So they went.

"He went out again about the sixth hour and the ninth hour and did the same thing. About the eleventh hour he went out and found still others standing around. He asked them, 'Why have you been standing here all day long doing nothing?'

"'Because no one has hired us,' they answered.
"He said to them, 'You also go and work in my vineyard.'

"When evening came, the owner of the vineyard said to his foreman, 'Call the workers and pay them their wages, beginning with the last ones hired and going on to the first.'

"The workers who were hired about the eleventh hour came and each received a denarius. So when those came who were hired first, they expected to receive more. But each one of them also received a denarius. When they received it, they began to grumble against the landowner. 'These men who were hired last worked only one hour,' they said, 'and you have made them equal to us who have borne the burden of the work and the heat of the day.'

"But he answered one of them, 'Friend, I am not being unfair to you. Didn't you agree to work for a denarius? Take your pay and go. I want to give the man who was hired last the same as I gave you. Don't I have the right to do what I want with my own money? Or are you envious because I am generous?'

"So the last will be first, and the first will be last."

The Reflection

Don't you just hate it when someone cuts in line? There you are, patiently standing in line while waiting to be served, then someone decides to cheat. Or do you give them the benefit of the doubt and assume that they just wandered innocently into the line or were in a personal emergency? Our first reaction isn't usually generous in these situations. This happened to me a few years back in New York. From where I was looking, I didn't see the extent of the line to get tickets for the subway; so I joined at what I thought was the end point. Within a New York second, a guy shouted at me to get to the back of the line! I was deeply embarrassed that people thought I was trying to muscle in, so I went to the back of the line without explanation—a condemned man!

The parable of the workers in the vineyard looks like it condones people jumping in line. "The last will be first, and the first will be last." If we look a little closer, though, not all is as it seems. Typically known as the parable of the workers in the vineyard, this parable has also been called the parable of the eccentric employer because the employer pays the workers in such an odd way. The landowner has hired throughout the day a number of men to work all at the same wage of one denarius— regardless of when they started work. He does not account for the number of hours the men have in fact labored, so those who started early and labored most of the day received the exact same wage as those who came along as dusk fell and worked many less hours. This is not normal economic practice; it is not "a fair wage for a fair day's work."

This parable has been linked directly to economic issues like unemployment, property ownership, and a "just" or "minimum" wage. This last point is the notion of a moral theory for determining wages so that people are paid according to a standard of what is a "fair," "living," or "sustainable" wage. These terms are all somewhat subjective, since the standard of living will be different in America compared to Rwanda, for example. What a large multinational company can pay in wage and benefits is quite different from what a Mom and Pop operation can pay.

The argument can be set against the backdrop of profit. Since wages affect the amount of profit to be had, they will soon enough become a factor in attacks on big business. The moral objection suggests that wages are set at the lowest level that big business can get away with. There is also the idea that surplus profit only goes to the big bosses, not to the workers. Set against this is the argument that higher wages make products more expensive, and if wages are too high then workers will be sourced in places or countries where labor is cheaper. As to surplus profit, the investors take the risks and should reap the reward.

Jesus assumes that the employer has the right to pay what he sees fit. Near the end of the workday, the landowner asks those who were standing around in the marketplace why they were not working; and they reply, "Because no one has hired us." So he hires them at a much more generous rate of pay than those who started first thing that morning, giving the workers in both groups a denarius. This comes close to the old joke about communism: "We'll pretend to work, and you pretend to pay us!" If this were applied to the economy today, we would soon see businesses close down. Where would the fairness be in that? In material terms, the employer in the parable is unjust in his payment arrangements. We can feel sympathy for those folks starting early and laboring all day only to find their employer, in his wisdom, paying the same wage to some Johnny-come-lately starting work as dusk begins to fall.

Yet this is exactly what God does. "For the kingdom of heaven is like a landowner who went out early in the morning to hire men to work in his vineyard." We are like those hired laborers, and God is like the owner of the vineyard. Jesus is telling us not to be like the resentful laborers. He reverses the understanding of how things work. His kingdom works differently than our world. He is not proposing this as the way to organize our labor practices. These contrasts underlie the difference between the two realms. Jesus concludes by pointing out that this is what the kingdom of heaven is like, not by saying, "And this is how you run a vineyard"!

The lesson we learn is that those who come late to faith are not at a disadvantage. Likewise, those who are involved in the church from birth are not advantaged. No one gets an automatic front seat in heaven! This is a hard teaching from Jesus. What he is telling us is that God rewards us with unexpected goodness. We are being warned and encouraged at the same time. It is a warning that we should not think we are above those outside of faith. To the contrary, we have a service to perform by bringing them to faith in Christ. It is encouraging because God is so generous in his offer of grace. We can think of the problem in another way. Should a parent love his or her children in different measures because one has been around longer than the other? Should the eldest child be loved more than the youngest? True parenting means loving each child as precious. God loves his children in this way.

The parable builds on the promises made by Jesus in earlier verses, when he promised us a place in heaven and assured us we will inherit everlasting life (see Matthew 7:33; 10:32, 39–42; 16:24–28; 18:3–4). In our economic life, promises are the basis of all our dealings; they are called contracts. When we buy a bus ticket, that ticket promises to deliver us to the stop we requested. It is the same with Jesus. He has promised to take us to our heavenly destination so long as we fulfill our side of the bargain by faithfully following him.

Jesus had already said, in essence, at the end of Matthew 19, that the first will be last and the last will be first. The parable leads to Jesus repeating the saying. It is such a hard lesson for the disciples that they have to ask again, prompting the parable. They still feel insecure in their place with God. Peter tells Jesus that he and his fellow disciples had to leave all to follow him. They want to understand what they will receive in return. They want to know what bargain is being struck. Jesus replies that their following him—these, the very first disciples—does not put them in a position of priority or advantage before God. God's reckoning is not about who did what first, who has done this or done that, how many of our good acts stack up against our bad acts. No, his response to our acts of faith is sheer grace, given with a generosity that we, like the first disciples, can hardly begin to fathom. We accept and we follow. We are in no position to bargain.

This is the great reversal—something we will encounter again and again in these parables—that Jesus declares. The rights of the first and last are being reversed. We are being shown the divine sense of equality, which is not about equal pay or human rights. It is about the divine right over us. The first and last are not to be thought of in sequence, the first then the last. It is clear in this parable that we all stand in equality before God's divine presence. Whether we are rich or poor, famous or obscure, politician or voter, executive or cashier, at life's end we all stand as equals in his court.

We are being warned of three specific things. First, we should not fall prey to a mentality of working for our wages, or "nickel-and-diming," in our spiritual affairs—with God or among ourselves. We are not to keep a spiritual set of accounts. Second, we should never fail to recognize God's sovereignty over us nor his right to distribute justice as he sees fit. Finally, we must distance ourselves from envy. What is most striking about this parable is the resentment of those who started work earlier in the day. In actuality, they got exactly what they had bargained for; the landowner did not cheat them in any way. The owner of the vineyard was prepared to hire laborers up to the last hour so that he could bring in the harvest, I would assume.

In one stroke Jesus has dismissed the human reckoning of how things should work. We should not presume salvation; it is God's to give, not ours to presume. The promise of faith should not lead to complacency. The Christian life is not like taking out an insurance policy that ensures us of heavenly riches. It is not a spiritual pension plan that guarantees heavenly comforts beyond this life. Our prayers are not accompanied by rights of admission.

The other side of the equation is the favor God is willing to give to those who have remained in darkness for so long, who have come to faith so much later in life. We should not be resentful of this. Instead, we should rejoice that we have labored so much longer in the Lord's vineyard; it is a much more satisfying lifestyle after all! On the other hand, Jesus does not invite us to pray Augustine's famous prayer: "O Lord, help me to be pure, but not yet!" God is no fool; we cannot assume that we can settle up with God before the day of judgment. Each of us has our journey of faith: we must follow when we are called, and we cannot tell the hour when he will call us home.

While we are working in the Lord's vineyard, we need to reflect on how we also function in the economic world. Few of us are waiting for a landowner to come and invite us to work as a day laborer. Ours is quite a different world. At the heart of the economic system is the company, which affects us directly as workers or indirectly as consumers. Companies can have more of a say in our lives than government, but they do not operate in a vacuum. They compete in the marketplace, driving toward profits and investments. We do not expect a company boss to come knocking on our door to offer us a denarius or a dollar to work in his office, store, or factory. Likewise, we do not expect everyone to earn the same. Our economic system is based on greater rewards for higher position, increased productivity, and other factors.

What does this mean for our "vocation"? Should we argue that Jesus is telling us that the world of work is organized wrongly? The answer to this is critical, as we seek to balance our life of faith with our work. We will spend, if we are in the workforce, some forty years or so working—eight hours a day, five days a week. This compares to perhaps an hour or two in church on Sunday and maybe a few hours a week in other church involvement or events. What is more important to us? What takes priority? If we are going to be "successful" in our work, we have to work hard to compete with others. Yet the more we work, the less time we have for our church and family—the heart of faithful living. The workplace is demanding to be sure; and our health can suffer, both our physical and spiritual health. Still, we need the money to support our family and to serve our church. How can we balance all of this?

The answer is buried in the text of our parable. The dissatisfaction, envy, and resentment of the workers all point to insecurity. We are not to be insecure in faith or jealous of others, when what we have is provided by God in his grace. As we look at our work world, we should be anchoring our attitude in his Word. This means not getting wrapped up in what others have. It means striving to fulfill the personal "vocation" we have in the economic world. This brings us personal rewards and rewards for our family, church, and community.

This is good discipleship in the economic world, although—like much of what we see in Jesus' parables—it is not easy. This is perhaps the hardest of teachings: the last will be first, and the first will be last. Jesus presents no abstract reflection; we face this challenge in the routine of our lives. When you see others enjoying a better lifestyle, when you hear about the extravagance of celebrities, or when you are tempted to envy a colleague receiving a promotion or recognition, then recall this hard teaching. Live sure in the knowledge that you are living a life of discipleship. Know that there is no place for resentment in the Christian life.

So the next time you see someone cutting in line, remember that you cannot react like that when it comes to understanding God's grace. We must have the faith and patience to see God's grace at work in all situations and places, however much we may feel cheated. Finally, if you do see someone jumping ahead of you, perhaps it will be me, and I have innocently strayed into your line.

Other Biblical Texts to Study

Matthew 20:1   Matthew 13:24–30; 21:28–46

Matthew 20:6–7   John 5:17; Romans 6:20–23

Matthew 20:8   Leviticus 19:13;
                      Deuteronomy 24:14–15

Matthew 20:12   James 1:11

Matthew 20:14	Ephesians 2:1–10; 2 Peter 3:8–9
Matthew 20:15	Deuteronomy 15:6–14; Mark 7:22; Luke 3:14
Matthew 20:16	Matthew 19:27–30; Mark 10:28–31; Luke 13:22–30

Things to Think About

- Recall a situation in which you felt envy. In the end, did things turn out differently than you expected? For example, did you find out the person was not as fortunate as you thought?

- Have you ever cut in line? Are there times when you have been undeservedly favored? How do you look back on those times now?

- Do you know individuals at school, work, church, or in your community who seem to have a privileged life? What sort of people are they? Is there something that stands between them and following Jesus?

- Are there other ways the last can be first and the first can be last? What sort of examples can you think of?

- What are your priorities? How can you create a better balance between your work and the rest of your life?

CHAPTER 5

CAN WE INVEST WISELY?

The Parable of the Ten Minas

LUKE 19:11–27

Introduction

Donald Trump once said that money is just the measure of how well he is playing the money game. We all organize our lives according to our income, but how do we measure success? This parable challenges us to think about trust and stewardship. It also warns us that God expects us to work with what we have and to be ambitious in our discipleship.

The Parable

While they were listening to this, he went on to tell them a parable, because he was near Jerusalem and the people thought that the kingdom of God was going to appear at once. He said: "A man of noble birth went to a distant country to have himself appointed king and then to return. So he called ten of his servants and gave them ten minas. 'Put this money to work,' he said, 'until I come back.'

"But his subjects hated him and sent a delegation after him to say, 'We don't want this man to be our king.'

"He was made king, however, and returned home. Then he sent for the servants to whom he had given the money, in order to find out what they had gained with it.

"The first one came and said, 'Sir, your mina has earned ten more.'

"'Well done, my good servant!' his master replied. 'Because you have been trustworthy in a very small matter, take charge of ten cities.'

"The second came and said, 'Sir, your mina has earned five more.'

"His master answered, 'You take charge of five cities.'

"Then another servant came and said, 'Sir, here is your mina; I have kept it laid away in a piece of cloth. I was afraid of you, because you are a hard man. You take out what you did not put in and reap what you did not sow.'

"His master replied, 'I will judge you by your own words, you wicked servant! You knew, did you, that I am a hard man, taking out what I did not put in, and reaping what I did not sow? Why then didn't you put my money on deposit, so that when I came back, I could have collected it with interest?'

"Then he said to those standing by, 'Take his mina away from him and give it to the one who has ten minas.'

"'Sir,' they said, 'he already has ten!'

"He replied, 'I tell you that to everyone who has, more will be given, but as for the one who has nothing, even what he has will be taken away. But those enemies of mine who did not want me to be king over them—bring them here and kill them in front of me.'"

The Reflection

This parable reminds me of Woody Allen's quip: "If only God would give me some clear sign! Like making a large deposit in my name in a Swiss bank." The parable of the ten minas, like many parables Jesus told, is a paradox. Taking it at face value, we might think that we can be productive servants simply by doing good deeds. The master gives each of his ten servants a capital sum of one mina, about three months' wages. Two of the servants invest their minas wisely and make a productive return on their investment. In regard to discipleship, this could suggest we can work our way to salvation by using our resources wisely—and woe to anyone who, like the third servant, is lazy and irresponsible.

Is this what Jesus was saying? Decidedly not. To see what was really being said, let us first make a few discoveries about the text.

First, the nobleman provides an allegory of the kingship of Christ. A "man of noble birth," he leaves to receive a kingdom. So the scene is set, but not for a revolution. The scene is set for Jesus' entry into Jerusalem. He is about to step into what we call Passion Week, culminating in the crucifixion and resurrection. Through the parable, we are being assured that he will return in judgment, reckon with his servants, and take vengeance on those who have denied him. The people were wondering about the coming of the kingdom, and they surely were wanting to understand what was to unfold in Jerusalem. Jesus dampens their eschatological ardor by talking about "a distant country." The poignancy of this parable is that it is told on the eve of Jesus' approach to Jerusalem, the city of messianic expectations.

Second, the nobleman summons his servants and gives each ten minas—putting them all on the same footing. The servants are to "do business." They are given an equal start, in contrast to the parable of talents in Matthew 25:14–30 where each servant is given according to his ability. There is no fixed profit target given to them, as confirmed by the acceptance of varying returns on the capital later in the parable. The message is that we are called to produce from what has been given to us and to be ready for the master's return. Obedience is to be our response to grace freely given.

Third, we need not worry about the value being used. The currency referred to is a mina, a Greek coin worth around one hundred drachmas at a time when a laborer would receive one drachma for a day's work. This is the only reference to a mina in the New Testament. What is essential here is the increase on what is given, the rate of productive return on the investment. That the amount appears small, especially compared to larger sums in the parable of the talents, indicates a test is to see if the servants are ready for greater tasks.

Finally, the servants refer to "your mina," the funds given by the nobleman. The servants have not earned the minas, so they are not theirs to use as such. The minas have been given to them to use in the best way they can, and the servants recognize that this is so.

This parable could be looked at in light of the Old Testament's ban on usury, the charging of interest. The biblical texts referred to are usually the laws set out in Deuteronomy and Leviticus, along with the condemnations of the prophets. The New Testament sheds little light on the subject. This parable, Jesus' words about lending in Luke 6:33–35, and the overturning of the tables of the money changers are key texts. The issue Jesus had with the money changers had more to do with *where* they were conducting business than with the nature of the business itself. There is no express condemnation of usury. In this parable Jesus does not choose to condemn usury either. Indeed, the one who has invested wisely at interest is the one who receives accolades in the story.

For the first fifteen hundred years of the church, charging interest was forbidden. It was John Calvin, by drawing a distinction between usury and interest, who changed all that. Interest became a legitimate charge on money, whereas usury was seen as an unfair or abusive use of interest, like loan sharking. Later theorists opposed to capitalism argued that this paved the way for capitalism, and the arguments are rehearsed to this day. If the Bible condemns the charging of interest, does this preclude a defense of capitalism? We'll say something about this question in the concluding chapter, but for now we can say that this parable does not offer conclusive evidence. Jesus had a quite different aim in mind.

This parable outlines what I would call a "faith economy." What is expected here is an act of discipleship. This means realizing our total dependence on God and knowing that it is not our act that brings about salvation, but God's action on us. This is true for all of humanity. The servants are all offered the same currency, in value and quantity. We learn that if we invest this currency wisely we will be accepted by the Lord and rewarded further. We also learn that this currency is given to us; we have not earned it. "Sir, *your* mina has earned" this return on investment. We receive this currency, and we are to invest it wisely for our Lord. The third servant is condemned because he hid the money rather than invest it. This servant said he was afraid of the master. Why? Was he afraid he would not do enough to share in any profit? He failed to trust in the outcome of the opportunity presented to him.

We can contrast this faith economy with our consumer economy. Consuming can be a restless activity of passing fashion and disposable products. Let's go back in time: Let's say we buy a video player. We like its modern design principles; it plays video tapes that we can rent or buy. We choose a Beta video player over a VHS player. If it breaks down, chances are we'll dispose of it rather than repair it. After a few years, video tapes and video players are replaced more and more by DVDs and DVD players, and so we go through the same consumption cycle. DVDs will go the same way. Who remembers Beta videos? Can you find Beta tapes or players in stores? The economy is driven by what we consume and how we consume. The key factors involved are insatiable desire, changing fashion, and developing technology. We can decide on how we value any product, which ultimately is disposable. Products come into being, they fulfill their purpose, and they pass into nothing.

We ourselves are an integral part of the consumer economy. We too are selling ourselves. We compete for jobs, position, and status in the economy. In order to compete, we have to market ourselves. Celebrities, like fashion clothing, are also in the category of sellable products. Pop stars come into fashion, fulfill their purpose, and pass into oblivion. (In some cases, we are grateful for their passing!) When Madonna cavorts on stage on a crucifix, her intention to shock sells because, unfortunately, there are buyers for this product. Supply and demand play their parts for individuals as much as objects or services.

The problem is not simply our consumption of products. We need to buy many basic things, such as food and clothing. Many of us need to buy a car to get to work; others need to buy train or bus tickets. There are things we enjoy buying, like books or music. We may want to spend money on an annual vacation. There is a myriad of choices in many of these decisions, limited only by our ability to pay. The real problem is when we allow our consumption and drive for status to define who we are. If the center of our being is selling ourselves, spending, and consuming—living by the American Express credit card slogan, "Don't leave home without it"—then we have a problem.

If we allow ourselves to become slaves to passing fashion, we will only find refuge in a hollow and restless experience. We need to work and to provide for our families, but we must not neglect our faith, family, friends, and church in the process. We cannot deny that the workplace is a competitive place and that the economy is a demanding environment. But we can wake up one day and find that the kids have grown up or that the church has closed down in our absence. If our work and the consumer demands upon us become the sole focus of our lives, then where does that leave us?

We can find meaning in the gospel, meaning that can be pivotal in our approach to working and consuming. The faith economy is quite a contrast to the consumer economy. The gospel is not disposable, though we are free to dispose of it for ourselves. We are free, spiritually speaking, to slide the gospel under the mattress, but we have to doubt the authenticity of such a faith. While the gospel may come in and out of life, it is never out of fashion. In short, the gospel is not biodegradable; it will persist. We can put it to one side, like the third servant in the parable did, but there will be no reward.

We do not choose *a* God; we choose *the* God. The gospel of Jesus Christ does not call for a choice to be made in the supermarket of faith; it is the gospel of the one and only God. In these days of cultural relativism and spiritual shopaholics, it is jarring to hear such statements of certainty. We are not supposed to talk like that. Yet how else are we to understand the God who says to Moses, "I am who I am"? Or Jesus when he says, "I am the way and the truth and the life"? This does not sound like *a* God, but *the* God—who has a claim on our lives.

The relationship here is not one of humanity to God, but of God to humanity. This is not about our decision to buy into faith; it is about our responding to the grace freely given by God. Lutheran theologian Gerhard Forde quotes a funny comment in a book he wrote on justification and grace. He writes about a controversial debate he attended. After the debate, "A nice old gentleman came shuffling up to me and said, 'You know, I can't figure it out. Why is it that when anyone talks about the sheer grace and absolute mercy of God, people get so mad?'"

Perhaps the old man can be answered by acknowledging that we feel deprived of our action. We are made powerless in the face of God's unconditional act. To accept God's grace does not make us sinless, nor do our actions become proof of perfection. On a superficial level it looks like we don't need to do anything at all, but would this be grace received? We have to doubt this. We are not paralyzed by grace, caught like believer rabbits in the headlamps of the divine light. The fact is that we do act, and our good actions or works become a reflection of the grace given by God and received in our hearts. What we do in faith is borne out of God's love for us and is part of our spiritual fabric.

To conclude with an analogy Forde used, in doing good we respond as a parent does to an injured child. If our child is injured, as parents we respond in love and with immediate action. Our decision to help is not premeditated. We do not act because we are intellectually convinced that this is the right thing to do or because it seems like a good idea. Our action is borne out of our love for our child. This is part of our fabric as a parent. This is instinctive to us, and we act in this sense without thinking.

Likewise, our acts of faith are instinctive of grace received. The issue here is not one of being a productive servant of Christ, but rather of being an active believer who in faith asks, "What shall I do?" We pick up the child, we care for the child, we love the child, and we do this because we know that this is what we are supposed to do.

Other Biblical Texts to Study

Luke 19:11	Matthew 25:14–30; Luke 18:31–34; Acts 1:6–8
Luke 19:12	Mark 13:32–37
Luke 19:14	Matthew 21:33–46; John 19:11–21; Acts 17:7
Luke 19:17	Proverbs 27:18; Luke 16:10
Luke 19:22	2 Samuel 1:16; Job 15:6; Hebrews 9:27
Luke 19:23	Matthew 21:12–13; Mark 11:15–17; John 2:14–16
Luke 19:26	Matthew 13:10–13; 25:28–29; Mark 4:25; Luke 8:18

Things to Think About

- Is there a parallel between this parable and how we earn money and consume today?

- Does Jesus endorse here the Jewish law prohibiting usury (the charging of interest), or has he changed the law?

- The Old Testament and the church forbade usury until the Reformation. How do you explain this apparent contradiction between Scripture and tradition?

- Is Jesus approving of the financial investments that are part and parcel of capitalism? How would you describe Jesus' attitude toward money?

- We hear a lot about a work/life balance. What would you say about a work/faith balance?

- How do you understand the relationship between faith and good works?

- Do you find the term "faith economy" helpful or confusing? If you find the term helpful, how would you extend it to explain your understanding of faith? If you find the term confusing, can you think of another concept that is more helpful to you?

CHAPTER 6

HOW SHOULD WE MANAGE OUR DEBTS?

The Parable of the Unmerciful Servant

MATTHEW 18:21–35

Introduction

The Old Testament forbade debt, yet Jesus seems to accept debt in this parable. Today's economy is heavily dependent on debt. Many people get deeply into debt, often ending up battling collection agencies if not declaring bankruptcy. What is the Christian's attitude toward debt? Should we be generous in helping people mired in debt?

The Parable

Then Peter came to Jesus and asked, "Lord, how many times shall I forgive my brother when he sins against me? Up to seven times?"

Jesus answered, "I tell you, not seven times, but seventy-seven times."

"Therefore, the kingdom of heaven is like a king who wanted to settle accounts with his servants. As he began the settlement, a man who owed him ten thousand talents was brought to him. Since he was not able to pay, the master ordered that he and his wife and his children and all that he had be sold to repay the debt.

"The servant fell on his knees before him. 'Be patient with me,' he begged, 'and I will pay back everything.' The servant's master took pity on him, canceled the debt and let him go.

"But when that servant went out, he found one of his fellow servants who owed him a hundred denarii. He grabbed him and began to choke him. 'Pay back what you owe me!' he demanded.

"His fellow servant fell to his knees and begged him, 'Be patient with me, and I will pay you back.'

"But he refused. Instead, he went off and had the man thrown into prison until he could pay the debt. When the other servants saw what had happened, they were greatly distressed and went and told their master everything that had happened.

"Then the master called the servant in. 'You wicked servant,' he said, 'I canceled all that debt of yours because you begged me to. Shouldn't you have had mercy on your fellow servant just as I had on you?' In anger his master turned him over to the jailers to be tortured, until he should pay back all he owed.

"This is how my heavenly Father will treat each of you unless you forgive your brother from your heart."

The Reflection

Have you seen that great Lending Tree ad on TV, where a guy is driving around a large yard on his lawn tractor, telling us all the great things he owns? At the end of the ad he asks the viewer, "How can I afford all this?" Then he looks directly into the camera and says cheerfully through gritted teeth, "Because

I'm in debt up to my eyeballs. I can barely pay my finance charges. Somebody help me!"

Debt is something that, in varying measures, nearly all of us have. We may have a mortgage, a car loan, credit card balances, or many other kinds of debt. The value of debt is that it can be used to leverage our earnings and investments—by financing big items and freeing up our monthly income for other things while some of the big items accrue in value beyond their original costs. A good example is our house and the improvements we make to it through financing loans, which enables us to use debt to increase our financial security and overall worth. However, debt can also be a liability that contributes to the loss of value in our investments, such as when a crash in the housing market occurs.

In the business world in general and on Wall Street in particular, debt is part of managing money. Governments and corporations issue bonds and stocks on the basis of their reputation. These are essentially debts that governments and companies create by borrowing money on the money markets. They have assets that they leverage by inviting investors to risk that they will not fail. This is why governments are the biggest borrowers because governments are considered too big to fail. Debt is issued to fund new research, projects, and expansion.

British economist John Maynard Keynes suggested that if you owe the bank a dollar you have a problem; but if you owe the bank a million dollars, then the bank has a problem. Brazil's finance minister a few years back added, "And if you're Brazil, then you own the bank!" U.S. banks had sunk so much money into Latin American economies that the reality was they were beholden to the finance ministers. They had to work out a deal to solve the debt crisis.

Individuals also borrow money against their assets, usually their home. And when you deposit your paycheck into the bank, you have created a debt, because the bank now owes you what you deposited. Your asset becomes the bank's liability. Your credit card debts, on the other hand, become the assets of your bank or card issuer. Our financial situation is tied to our reputation for keeping up with these payments because our borrowing power is based on our previous record of repaying loans or bills.

The fragility of debt is a big picture and small picture thing. The big picture is that we may be living in an economic bubble, and history teaches us that all economic bubbles burst. If this happens, many of us will be in deep trouble. The small picture is that people also experience their own personal bubble. The bubble bursts when they lose their job, get a divorce, and so on. Meanwhile everyone is carrying on business as usual. Debt, essentially, is a relational issue. If you run into trouble, your best recourse is to talk to your creditors. They can help you plan a way out of the problem.

If we ignore our debt we can get drawn into its centrifugal force, swallowed up by higher interest payments. We can get manipulated by loan sharks, becoming hopelessly mired in debt and in need of rescue. The problem is not interest per se, but the abuse of the charges. If you act responsibly, you can manage your debt. If you get drawn in too deep, however, then you will be open to abuse.

The question of interest was no different when Jesus told this parable. He used an example of someone in a lot of debt—definitely up to his eyeballs! The sum Jesus uses is vast on purpose. Ten thousand talents, millions of dollars, was clearly too much for the servant to repay the king. He has little to fall back on, and even selling himself and his wife and children into slavery will not fix the problem. All the man can do is beg to be released from the debt, which the king does with compassion. What does the forgiven servant do in response? Unrepentant for his own indebtedness, he demands one hundred denarii owed by a fellow servant. This is such a trivial amount compared to his own debt, yet he has the other servant thrown into jail until he could repay the debt. Such ingratitude!

We learn the real value of forgiveness in this parable. We can look around us and see all the wonderful things we have. We can wonder at the world created to sustain us. We can stand in awe at the marvelous things God has given us. We can turn to ourselves and see how little we have to give in return. Yet God does not demand much from us, only that we give ourselves to him in faith. This is the set of spiritual accounts God keeps with us, and we are up to our eyeballs in debt!

Why does Jesus tell us this story to explain forgiveness? Because, as 1 Timothy 6:10 says, "The love of money [the *love of money*, not money itself as some folks misquote Paul] is a root of all kinds of evil." If we love money or possessions too much, then we will never be generous with them. We will try to hold on to our money and possessions more than we hold on to Christ. Jesus knows this. He knows what hold our money and possessions have on us.

If we have enough money and possessions, then we are more able to be generous. We see how wealthy people can be generous by running charity events and setting up foundations. It is good they do this work. However—and with Jesus there is always a *however*—such generosity will not buy the wealthy a place at the Lord's table. Only faith can do that. Faith will also make us generous, no matter how little we may have. Remember the widow's mite? How little she had, yet how generous she was with so little.

Generosity is relative—like a man with a hole in his shoe is better off than a man with no shoes. We read in Romans 13:8: "Let no debt remain outstanding, except the continuing debt to love one another." We need to look beyond our problems and our self-absorbed view of our situation and in love look to others and how they live. We can easily fool ourselves into being less than generous. We can pretend that someone wealthier, with less money hassles, will help the poor. We can also think that all the solutions will come from someone else because we are too wrapped up in our own problems.

What we ought to be doing is looking at how we might help others with their debt. This can be done by helping those in our own family with their problems, offering to help a neighbor, or volunteering through our church or a community group to offer debt counseling. More than having money given to them, many people just need help to find a solution before they fall deeper into debt. In some cases, being generous with our time can be far more valuable than being generous with our money.

How do our concerns look when compared to the generosity of God's grace? When we forget to pray? When we forget to give thanks or acknowledge that we owe all to God? When we turn away from the generosity he shows us? When we do not share this knowledge of him? When we do not use our gifts and experience to serve him in the world? At times like these, we are like the servant who demands his one hundred denarii. Our demands cost the King dearly. The price of God's grace was the life of his Son, Jesus Christ. How cheaply we turn from him when we deny that we owe all to him.

The Bible opens with the account of God as creator of all that is in the world. We read of our broken relationship with him. When we give him praise, then we acknowledge that he is the creator God. When we give him thanks, we acknowledge that he is the one who has been generous to us. When we submit ourselves to him, we acknowledge our debt to him. When we act as if we did it all ourselves and deny others a share of his generosity, then we turn away from him in sin.

The opposite of generosity is greed. Theologians who criticize the free enterprise system often assume that greed is what makes capitalism work. They argue that greed is part of the "sinful structure" of the free market. This suggests that all people in the free market economy act greedily, except presumably those who advocate such a view! Their argument avoids the fact that greed is about people, not structures. People can be greedy for things economic or noneconomic. While there are many greedy people, the majority are just trying to get by.

What the great classical economic writers put at the center of the free market system is not greed but self-interest. This is where there is confusion. Doing the self-interested thing is not the same as doing the selfish thing. A few years back I met a guy on a train who had gambled away his house, marriage, and family. He was pretty much broke. Do you know where he was going? Back to the racetrack! We can spend our money on gambling, a selfish indulgence. It is not in our self-interest economically; like this fellow, we could lose everything.

The ambition of the gambler is to buy security and happiness in one giant leap. The ambition of the Christian is to receive God's grace, which cannot be bought cheaply. God's grace has already been bought for us on the cross. In Christ alone we find our ambition. Eric Liddell, the Scottish runner turned missionary, said that when he ran he felt God's pleasure. When we are succeeding, achieving things, we too can feel God's pleasure. When we live in Christ—knowing that we are up to our eyeballs in debt—when we acknowledge that what we do is for God, when we turn to help others out of their debt, then we will feel God's pleasure.

Other Biblical Texts to Study

Matthew 18:21	Matthew 18:15; Luke 17:3–4
Matthew 18:22	Genesis 4:24
Matthew 18:27	Luke 7:40–43
Matthew 18:28–30	Deuteronomy 15:1–11
Matthew 18:33	Matthew 6:12; Romans 13:8; Colossians 3:12–13; Ephesians 4:32
Matthew 18:35	Matthew 6:14–15

Things to Think About

- How do you manage your debts? Do you set rules or limits for borrowing and lending?

- Is a debt always a bad thing? Can it be a tool if we use it wisely?

- What do you make of Paul's words in Romans 13:8: "Let no debt remain outstanding, except the continuing debt to love one another"? How strictly and literally should we take this verse?

- Can you recall an occasion when you were generous? Can you recall an occasion when you were unforgiving? How did you feel on each occasion?

- Why do you think people get into debt? Should others help them? How can they help themselves?

- What do you think about all the advertising that encourages us to take advantage of using credit? Does it make us aware of legitimate opportunities or try to manipulate us?

- Do you think people in deep debt are best served by having their debts canceled? What message does this send to people about falling into debt?

- Can Jesus' words in this parable and elsewhere be extended to "forgiving the debts" of poor countries? You might want to study this question in conjunction with chapter 9 on the parable of the two debtors (Luke 7:40–50).

- Do you think greed is what makes the free enterprise system work? If so, what do you think can be done to change the way the economy works?

- Do you agree that greed needs to be distinguished from self-interest? How can you apply this to your own life?

CHAPTER 7

THE THINGS WE HAVE, WHOSE ARE THEY?

The Parable of the Rich Fool

LUKE 12:13–21

Introduction

We all know that, in the end, "You can't take it with you!" But in this parable Jesus tells us that it's not all ours to "take" in the first place. It all belongs to God. We cannot find salvation or comfort in the things we own, though people often act as if they can. Does our wealth create a personal barrier to faith? Or do we only think of other people as wealthy?

The Parable

Someone in the crowd said to him, "Teacher, tell my brother to divide the inheritance with me."

Jesus replied, "Man, who appointed me a judge or an arbiter between you?" Then he said to them, "Watch out! Be on your guard against all kinds of greed; a man's life does not consist in the abundance of his possessions."

And he told them this parable: "The ground of a certain rich man produced a good crop. He thought to himself, 'What shall I do? I have no place to store my crops.'

"Then he said, 'This is what I'll do. I will tear down my barns and build bigger ones, and there I will store all my grain and my goods. And I'll say to myself, "You have plenty of good things laid up for many years. Take life easy; eat, drink and be merry."'

"But God said to him, 'You fool! This very night your life will be demanded from you. Then who will get what you have prepared for yourself?'

"This is how it will be with anyone who stores
up things for himself but is not rich toward God."

The Reflection

Do you know the words of that old Janis Joplin song?

Oh Lord, won't you buy me a Mercedes Benz?
My friends all drive Porsches, I must make amends.

We often hear that we live in a very materialistic age. In our consumer culture, to have is to be. I consume; therefore I am. As we go throughout the day, we periodically check our cell phone if it hasn't rung out the latest downloadable tune—making sure that we're still connected to the world, still wanted. We have become consumers of news, seduced by salacious gossip or violent crimes rather than informed about what we need to know as responsible citizens. The news outlets pander to this consumer demand by offering "news" that they deem we want and condescending editorials about what we are supposed to think. Critics of the free market system believe that materialism is an essential element of the system. They argue that the drive toward materialism is a necessary, and evil, outcome of free market activity. The question they need to ask, however, is whether this is a true picture of the economy. They need to look more closely at the difference between consumption and consumerism.

We can classify our purchases into three basic categories: necessities, additional comforts, and unnecessary items. We need to buy food to live, but how much—and of what kind—do we need to live on? We might argue we need a car, but how comfortable does it need to be? We could get by driving a Ford or a Saturn rather than a Mercedes or a Porsche. Most of us buy many things that we don't really need, things like new CD players, jewelry, and the latest fashion in clothes.

We all draw the line on our spending according to our means. However well this book sells, I don't think it will give me the income to buy a diamond-studded dog collar, even if I wanted to (and even if I had a dog)! Paris Hilton is no doubt in a different situation. We are treated daily to the antics of the wealthy and celebrities of the world. We can only stand in awe at the seemingly endless things that money can buy, if we have the wealth to buy them. In contrast, we can only wince at the daily struggles of those too poor to pay for the basic necessities of life.

In the divine economy, Jesus turns this all on its head. However well we may be doing in life, this parable puts our situation in stark relief, as God declares: "This very night your life will be demanded from you. Then who will get what you have prepared for yourself?" We can spend a lifetime in the pursuit of material comfort, storing up wealth in the form of our house, the things we hold precious within it, our cars, and all manner of other things. Yet, at the very hour our life is demanded, what becomes of them?

The setting of the parable is a man asking Jesus to rule on an inheritance dispute between himself and his brother. Most likely this was a younger brother who had a grievance against the oldest son in the family, who typically received a double portion of the father's estate (see Deuteronomy 21:17). This younger brother probably wanted to collect his share and become independent, but the oldest had refused because he wanted their father's inheritance to remain all together. Such disputes would usually be resolved by appeal to a rabbi. Jesus responds by asking the man where he got the idea that Jesus should resolve the matter. Jesus has in mind a much bigger issue than this one dispute.

Wanting to convey the spiritual dangers of wealth and covetousness, Jesus tells the parable of the rich fool. The rich man in this simple story has a problem: How can he store the excess grain from this harvest's bumper crop? He is not worried about his wealth deserting him because he believes he is set for life. He has every confidence that he can enjoy his wealth, sit back, and rejoice in the plenty. He does this without regard for neighbor or God. This is an attitude of folly! God enters the story and addresses him directly, confronting him with a crisis: "You fool! This very night your life will be demanded from you."

The rich man's wealth has no value before God because, in the crisis of judgment, the rich man cannot take his wealth with him. Because of the fall of humanity, our relationship with God has been broken; acquiring wealth will not restore our broken relationship with God, will not gain us entry into heaven. What God demands in our discipleship is trust and obedience. The reward of discipleship is freedom from the greed that accompanies the bondage to material possessions.

In the teachings of Jesus, we find a number of references to money and wealth as an obstacle to true discipleship and relationship with God. This is particularly true in the case of Luke's Gospel. Jesus warns of the spiritual threat if we put money first, since we cannot serve both God and money (Luke 16:13). He tells us not to pursue wealth idolatrously (Luke 12:31–34) and that we should give freely (Luke 6:30; 11:41; 14:12–14; 18:22; 19:8). In all of these teachings, Jesus offers us images of forgiveness and the restoration of relationship with God.

Jesus tells us that not only will we find being materialistic a barrier for entry into the kingdom of heaven, but also the poor will get there first. This is a dangerous path to tread, however, because we don't want to suggest that the poor would be better off left alone to die poor. We cannot entertain this thought for a moment because our responsibility is to help others who are poor. The poor can receive riches before which all other values fade (Matthew 13:44–46). They can experience the great hope of a God who accepts them, even though they are empty-handed.

The early church father Theodoret wrote, "He has sent me to preach glad tidings to the poor." Theodoret suggested that this poverty is spiritual because human nature has fallen into extreme poverty and has become enslaved to idols. This understanding was echoed by other early church fathers, such as Cyril, who wrote that the "poor are those who lack all goodness, who have no hope, and who are without God."

Jesus wants us to understand spiritual poverty and to see that from this flows poverty in other areas of life. What we learn from this parable is that ultimately we all go empty-handed before God. We will be judged on our faith, not on our bank balance. If we are spiritually strong, then we understand that all we have can be put to the purposes of God. In short, that is discipleship. The parable calls us to trust in God, not in material wealth, and to know that all is owed to God.

This does not mean we enter a "spirituality only zone," a place where all the problems of the world are excluded or excused. We live in the tension between our own free will and the call to obedience to God. The battle is between the old Adam and the new Adam. We pursue our relationship with God in both a spiritual and physical dimension. To go in only one of these two directions is to be lopsided in our faith. We say yes to Jesus, and from this flows our acts of faith in the world.

This will lead us away from the pursuit of material gain and toward a better understanding of how we can serve God. In the economic sense, this means having a responsibility toward our neighbor. In America, and in a globalized world, we may well ask: *Who is my neighbor?* The good Samaritan may be traveling on a transcontinental airline flight rather than walking along a rural path. We have the poor in our own nation as well as on the other side of the world. Despite this, we should not forget the basic commandment to love our neighbor, which can be applied as much in a globalized world as in Jesus' day.

In the global economy we are all interconnected. The emergence of globalization offers opportunities and threats for all of us, like any major shift in human understanding and behavior. Naturally, there is debate surrounding the question of whether the impact of globalization is good or bad. One benefit of globalization is that we can experience cultures across the world so much more easily. Business translates this into new markets, cheaper labor, and production closer to overseas markets. This creates opportunities for creating wealth in poorer developing countries as entrepreneurial local businesses support foreign businesses in their country.

Protestors contend that this leads to abuse in poorer countries—an argument based on their deeply rooted suspicion of business, which is an outgrowth of their political ideology. They present a world where businesspeople live a Jekyll and Hyde existence as they travel from home to work, from home market to foreign market. At home they are trusted citizens of the state, which is a force for good. But at work they are corporate monsters, a force for evil.

Certainly some companies are abusing conditions in less-developed countries; but then again they are often in league with corrupt middlemen and governmental officials. A major barricade to economic development in poorer countries is corruption at all levels of government. Resources intended to help the poor get poured into other unrelated government projects or into some bureaucrat's offshore bank account. Tackling corruption and attempting to implement good economic practices is now tied to financing in developing countries, but the protestors only retort that this results in enslavement of these economies.

The option in these countries is now clear: governments and businesses need to clean up and gear up, or the poor will get poorer. There does not appear to be a choice for the protestors. Believing that giving more and more money to poor countries will solve their problems, they want us to throw good money after bad. But this is naive at best and destructive at worst.

Any healthy economy demands hard decisions and requires sensible management, including regulation that is not cumbersome and does not stifle entrepreneurs and new business initiatives. This is how free markets grow. Much of this can be achieved without recourse to moral arguments. Yes, the moral demands on individuals are constant, and they require us to face a crisis of decision about how we are going to live, spend, and invest. However, this is not an issue regarding the modern economic system per se; these decisions are to be taken in response to God's demand on us and our hope for salvation.

Governments, businesses, and other market organizations are not instruments of salvation nor are they institutions in league with the devil. They are the means by which we can cooperate in a global marshalling of people and resources in a conflict of wants, needs, and beliefs—moral or otherwise. We alone ultimately stand before God and are called to account for what we have done and for what we have left undone. We alone can show God where we have placed our heart.

There have been attempts in recent years to join the Christian message to anti-globalization and anti-capitalist rhetoric. We see this protest theology joining other protest ideologies. By doing this, Christians are turning Jesus into a secular political campaigner. To do this is to lose Christ crucified, Christ the Son of God, who overcame death in order to give us new life. We end up with Jesus as just another politician, another good man, another lost voice in the pantheon of well-intentioned political leaders.

The voice of faith is lost in such protest. It becomes lost in the secular melee of voices in the marketplace of ideas. Our challenge is ultimately an individual one, not one involving a collective consciousness that brings salvation here on earth. In a materialist understanding of the world, it is as if there is no afterlife. It is as though there is no God to judge us or others. It is to decide there is no heavenly place awaiting us and all those who have been burdened in this world. It is to fail to hear God when he says, "You fool! This very night your life will be demanded from you. Then who will get what you have prepared for yourself?"

Other Biblical Texts to Study

Luke 12:14	Micah 6:8; Romans 2:1–3; 9:20
Luke 12:15	1 Timothy 6:6–10
Luke 12:19	Ecclesiastes 11:9; Isaiah 22:12–14; 1 Corinthians 15:32
Luke 12:20	Job 27:8–10; Psalm 39:6–11; Jeremiah 17:11; Luke 11:39–41
Luke 12:21	Matthew 6:19–21; Luke 12:32–34

Things to Think About

- How do you define wealth? How do you feel about your wealth and how you acquire it?

- Is consumerism a bad thing? Do you see a difference between consumerism and consumption?

- When does our attitude toward wealth and consuming create a barrier between us and God?

- As part of faithful discipleship, how should we change our ideas about wealth? Can you name three things you could change today? If so, how could you change them?

- Do you worry too much about paying your bills and about your job security? Is it tempting to think you are at the mercy of economic forces beyond your control—beyond even God's control?

- Is it possible for a Christian to be rich *and* a good disciple? Is there a threshold of wealth that a Christian cannot cross?

- Do you think it is more difficult to be a disciple in today's economy than in the economy of Jesus' time? What differences are there between the two situations?

- Do you think churches and theologians are too negative about globalization and the free enterprise system? What should they be telling people with plenty of money?

CHAPTER 8

HOW PRODUCTIVE ARE WE?

The Parable of the Tenants

MATTHEW 21:33–46

Introduction

Jesus calls us to be productive servants—as individuals and as the church. We are given gifts to bring fullness to our faith and life. This has implications for how we run our households and how we are to care for our community.

The Parable

"Listen to another parable: There was a landowner who planted a vineyard. He put a wall around it, dug a winepress in it and built a watchtower. Then he rented the vineyard to some farmers and went away on a journey. When the harvest time approached, he sent his servants to the tenants to collect his fruit.

"The tenants seized his servants; they beat one, killed another, and stoned a third. Then he sent other servants to them, more than the first time, and the tenants treated them the same way. Last of all, he sent his son to them. 'They will respect my son,' he said.

"But when the tenants saw the son, they said to each other, 'This is the heir. Come, let's kill him and take his inheritance.' So they took him and threw him out of the vineyard and killed him.

"Therefore, when the owner of the vineyard comes, what will he do to those tenants?"

"He will bring those wretches to a wretched end," they replied, "and he will rent the vineyard to other tenants, who will give him his share of the crop at harvest time."

Jesus said to them, "Have you never read in the Scriptures:

"'The stone the builders rejected
   has become the capstone;

the Lord has done this,
   and it is marvelous in our eyes'?

"Therefore I tell you that the kingdom of God will be taken away from you and given to a people who will produce its fruit. He who falls on this stone will be broken to pieces, but he on whom it falls will be crushed."

When the chief priests and the Pharisees heard Jesus' parables, they knew he was talking about them. They looked for a way to arrest him, but they were afraid of the crowd because the people held that he was a prophet.

The Reflection

The environment was not a hot topic when I was growing up. The biggest environmental worry back in the 1960s and 1970s was that the world was cooling. Experts were predicting that the earth would be four degrees cooler by 1990 and eleven degrees cooler by 2000. The fear was that there would be a new ice age. Well, that hasn't happened. Instead, the new fear is global warming. Who is to say what new fears we will have twenty or thirty years from now?

What does this have to do with economics? Many environmental groups argue that free market capitalism is causing irreparable damage to the environment. They also contend that the world is overpopulated, a claim that has surfaced on a regular basis since the Rev. Thomas Malthus first made it two hundred years ago. And they say we are running out of fuel, which has a lot to do with economics.

Global warming, waste recycling, and escalating gas prices get a great deal of media attention. Concern for the environment has spawned a vast movement, with an industry and public policy bureaucracy of its own. There are two broad secular views of the environment. Environmental interest groups argue that humanity has caused serious problems—many of which they contend are created by manufacturing, commerce, and rampant consumerism—for ourselves and future generations. They lobby for changes that they believe will slow the destruction of the planet. The other view, held by many in the scientific community, is that new technological developments and economic change will resolve our difficulties. Those who take this more optimistic position believe that this has always been the way humanity has overcome problems. Both views are aware of the difficulties but have different policy options to offer.

Christians have also taken an interest in the debate. Liberal theologians tend to get on board with the environmental lobbyists more readily than with the alternative view. However, they see the underlying concerns connecting with theological ideas: God has given us dominion over the earth, and we are to take care of our world. Many in the environmental interest groups and scientific community don't quite share this view. They would dismiss this theological view as too anthropocentric because it puts humanity rather than a broader understanding of nature at the center, which they say is why we messed up the world in the first place.

A concern for the environment is now being linked by some evangelical Christian lobbies to the biblical call to stewardship. We confess that God is the creator of all things in heaven and earth. All that we have belongs to him as the owner of creation, and ultimately we are made to be with God. We have stewardship of the world for a short time, until we are called home.

From Christianity's inception, Christians have understood that the world is God's creation and that we have been given a stewardship role within it. This seems to be what links different theological positions to the issue of environmentalism. Let us then use this parable to probe a little deeper and see if God's Word contains an eco-theology.

Our starting point has to be that our view of the world is God-centered. God is the creator and sustainer of this world. God has given us stewardship of the world, making us tenants, never owners. If we look at the vast differences in human values and approaches to life, then it is difficult to see how stewardship is to work in practice. In environmental terms, we end up with the contradictions of countries giving environmental aid on the one hand and ammunition to fight costly and destructive wars on the other. If anything can help humanity to sustain life, it is freedom and peaceful coexistence.

In facing this complexity, we find "environmental fundamentalism" screaming out, "The sky is falling! The sky is falling!" Theories of global warming are largely that—theories. This is not to say they are necessarily wrong; they may be correct. But there are opposing theories, and in time we may find that an alternative view is the correct one. Remember that not long ago we were expecting an ice age. Global warming theories are based on incomplete scientific models. At the end of the nineteenth century some people were predicting the depletion of coal and the end of the world's energy resources. This scenario, of course, did not take place.

Either we have finite means—which will one day run out unless we stop using them—or we do not. In reality, we don't know what quantity of resources we have. Nor do we know what future generations will discover and innovate for themselves. To take a defensive view, as do the environmental activists, is to ignore the fact that human ingenuity and economic resourcefulness continually take us in new directions. This is why we can look back and smile at the predictions that our forebearers made.

In the economic arena, a problem with the environmental interest groups is that they have been long on grand theories but short on economic data. They are unable to measure environmental impact in any meaningful economic way. The way to address effective stewardship of the environment will involve a combination of scientific knowledge and the economic organization needed to make change—for our generation and the future.

What this really involves is a disagreement about the public policies needed to sustain our world. The question is not *whether* we should look after the world, but *how*. There are many forces at work, with conflicting vested interests, and they will determine where the debate goes in the future. Being suspicious of free enterprise in the first place, some will not accept that big business has a positive role to play in all this. These protestors see themselves as advocates of the weak against the strong, supporters of the humble of the earth against the powerful corporations. They picture big business as cynically ravaging the earth's resources, wicked tenants writ large.

This brings us to the parable.

Jesus' starting point, which we see in Matthew 21:31–32, is that the gospel is offered to the poor in spirit "the tax collectors and the prostitutes." Likewise, the end point is that the kingdom of God is taken away from the religious elite and given "to a people who will produce its fruit" (Matthew 21:43). As so often in the Gospels, the chief priests and the Pharisees are held up as a foil of power and position. This is because the gospel is rejected by the leaders of the community, who are in reality fearful. The powerful prefer to keep the humble just where they are, and they fear the crowds.

The wicked tenants recognize the rightful heir, but they subvert this knowledge by casting him outside the vineyard and killing him. The fear of the crowd in the Gospels is the fear of those who recognized, at least to some degree, who Jesus was and that he was bringing about a different order of things. Likewise for those who hear God's Word today. Jesus has already answered our problems, but continually he is cast out and killed. Each time someone dies in poverty, Christ is cast out. Each time we put our own desires before God's demand on us, Christ is cast out. We then live as if Jesus did not die for us. We trivialize his death each time we think we know best. We too can be Pharisees; we too can fear the crowd.

God has provided for us, carefully so, but still we squabble over what he has given us. Greed for money, power, and position distances people from the good maintenance of the vineyard that God has provided for us. Daily we reject the offer to the humble; and in so doing we reject our own potential for humility, our need to be humbled. The human will power emphasizes our desire to maximize our utility, our material well-being. Only when we embrace the servanthood of Christ can we overcome this will and truly maximize selfhood.

Economic life, in part, is about aspirations. How are we to balance our economic goals with our aspiration to be with Christ? We can't secure this using plastic—"gold," "platinum," or otherwise. We cannot allow ourselves to be seduced by slick marketing that seeks to offer us materialistic salvation. This is an aspect of the economy that we must battle with, but the battle is within ourselves. Other facets of our economic life are our work, mortgage, other debts, investments, and relationships with other economic agents. These are the day-to-day realities of living in the economy. We struggle with them, and we calculate and measure our daily life by them.

Those who would want to undermine the free market system are escapists. They too have economic aspirations. This protest movement has its own style of dress, music, and language, branded and sold like any other commodity in the economic world. The celebrities who preach to us about the ills of free enterprise earn huge advertising contracts from major companies. They are, in effect, the chief executive officers of multi-million-dollar-a-year corporations, something along the line of "U2 Inc." and the "George Clooney Corporation." They are what they protest.

The crowds who gather to protest free enterprise and globalization warn us of environmental cynicism and poor stewardship and link these to poverty. Are they the crowds to be feared? I suggest not. The crowd Jesus faced was not a group of well-heeled protestors in designer jeans, organized via the Internet. They did not cheer rock stars with wealth beyond their dreams at "poverty concerts." The crowds who gather to protest capitalism are what they protest. They fly to the protests using cheap Internet airline deals, seek the best hotel packages, and wear designer clothes. They seek identity in this economy, a cause that will set them apart, showing themselves to be radically different from people in business suits or doing an honest day's work. Where is the prophecy in that?

The protestors have become, in essence, "consumers of poverty," purchasing the feel-good factor of thinking that they have done something about the problem. Poverty is deeply troubling and complex, with many causes and with many barriers standing in the way of change. Many of the environmental problems are in poorer countries, which do not have the economic resources to tackle their difficulties. One effect of better economic management in these countries will be better environmental conditions. There are people in poor countries who can help themselves; they need the capital to invest and the know-how, not sympathy.

The powerful at the G8, World Bank, World Trade Organization, and a host of others who meet to tackle poverty are well aware of poverty. They can provide the required capital and know-how. There is an arrogance in the assumption that they cannot—an arrogance that is often the hallmark of celebrities used to doors being opened for them or of the youth who believe they know better.

The leaders of the G8 have the task of weighing the wants of their own nation with the wants of the other nations of the world. Governments have a first-order task to look after their citizens, and that means us. The Pharisees are not other people; they are all of us. Our economic life is one of self-maximization, and it reflects what we are. The economy, a product of our will, is what we are. Any organization led by sinful people will end up as a sinful edifice—not because it is a sinful construct, but rather because organizations are run by sinful people.

There are many demands on our wealth. Our church needs money, charities need money, yet is our giving relative to our wealth? Let us draw a comparison. A new music CD costs around fifteen dollars (and if you try to download pirated material, the lawyers of celebrities will be quickly in pursuit). Do you give to the church or charity with the same generosity as you do for your own desires? Yet, in church what do you consume? You "consume" Christ. You stand in the presence of the one who can give you eternal life, not just a few moments of pleasure. Jesus gives himself freely, yet even in the face of this gift we choose selfishness.

The Christian community, in its prophetic ministry, is not to be a refuge for selfish souls. As local churches, communities of sinners, we abide in Christ, the vine (see John 15:1–17). The vine is the noblest of plants. It needs much care to grow and flourish, to bear its fruit. It spreads, winding its way carefully over a long time, able to cling to the trellis of the vineyard for support and to offer us shade. It produces the fruit that becomes the grape of the Lord's Supper. The contents of the soil are infused into the grape, so unpredictable that it yields differently under different conditions. In the Lord's Supper, the influences of the earth, of God's creation, find their way into the grape, into the fluid, and into the chalice to be consumed in the name of our Lord Jesus Christ. We are at that moment connected to the totality of God's creation. In that moment we are to die to ourselves and to live in Christ. This is our calling.

As we ponder the ills of society—environmental destruction, millions of people dying in poverty, the wars of the world—then we should ponder also the world we have tended. We are what we protest. In response to our prophetic call in Christ, we can best answer practically by our "yes" to Christ: our willingness to serve and our willingness to change for his sake. When we change, a little more of the world changes; and the crowd that is feared grows by another soul turned to Christ.

Other Biblical Texts to Study

Matthew 21:33	Psalm 80:8–19; Isaiah 5:1–7; Mark 12:1–12; Luke 20:9–19 ●
Matthew 21:41	Acts 13:44–48; 18:5–6; 28:25–28
Matthew 21:42	Psalm 118:22–23; Acts 4:8–12; Ephesians 2:19–20; 1 Peter 2:4–8
Matthew 21:43	1 Peter 4:10; 1 Corinthians 4:1–5
Matthew 21:44	Isaiah 8:13–15; Romans 9:30–33
Matthew 21:46	Matthew 21:10–11

Things to Think About

- Are protestors right to protest globalization, or does this represent narrow political interests at work?

- Do you believe the environment and poverty are linked? In what ways?

- Is the reality of people dying in poverty a judgment on humanity? Is this Christ being "cast out"?

- Do you agree that those opposed to free enterprise are escapists?

- Do we have the economic world we deserve? How could we make the world a better place economically?

- How do you view your personal economic life in contrast to the poverty in the world?

CHAPTER 9

CAN WE FORGIVE DEBTS?

The Parable of the Two Debtors

LUKE 7:36–50

⌒

Introduction

The forgiveness of debts, applied to debts owed by poor nations to rich nations, has become a political policy. This idea is based on texts in Leviticus related to the Year of Jubilee. There are problems with viewing forgiveness in this way. This parable and the story surrounding it show us what Jesus really means by forgiveness—that is, that it is a concept outside the realm of economics.

The Parable

Now one of the Pharisees invited Jesus to have dinner with him, so he went to the Pharisee's house and reclined at the table. When a woman who had lived a sinful life in that town learned that Jesus was eating at the Pharisee's house, she brought an alabaster jar of perfume, and as she stood behind him at his feet weeping, she began to wet his feet with her tears. Then she wiped them with her hair, kissed them and poured perfume on them.

When the Pharisee who had invited him saw this, he said to himself, "If this man were a prophet, he would know who is touching him and what kind of woman she is—that she is a sinner."

Jesus answered him, "Simon, I have something to tell you."

"Tell me, teacher," he said.

"Two men owed money to a certain moneylender. One owed him five hundred denarii, and the other fifty. Neither of them had the money to pay him back, so he canceled the debts of both. Now which of them will love him more?"

Simon replied, "I suppose the one who had the bigger debt canceled."

"You have judged correctly," Jesus said.

Then he turned toward the woman and said to Simon, "Do you see this woman? I came into your house. You did not give me any water for my feet, but she wet my feet with her tears and wiped them with her hair. You did not give me a kiss, but this woman, from the time I entered, has not stopped kissing my feet. You did not put oil on my head, but she has poured perfume on my feet. Therefore, I tell you, her many sins have been forgiven—for she loved much. But he who has been forgiven little loves little."

Then Jesus said to her, "Your sins are forgiven."

The other guests began to say among themselves, "Who is this who even forgives sins?"

Jesus said to the woman, "Your faith has saved you; go in peace."

The Reflection

Words often become fashionable or are put to work in different ways—particularly in the heat and emotion of public debate. This is difficult for biblical words in our modern age because we want them to mean specific things about God. This does not stop biblical words from being picked up and devalued in a secular context, thereby becoming casualties of secular debate. Forgiveness is such a word. For example, "Forgive me for saying this" often actually means "Boy, are you wrong!" Forgiveness has become a fashionable word, employed by lobbies seeking to tackle the wrongs of the past such as war crimes and slavery, as well as other causes.

A popular application of *forgiveness* in the past decade has come from the campaign to erase the debts owed by poorer nations to richer nations. Many groups, both secular and Christian, have put pressure on governments, especially in America and Britain, to "forgive" these debts. The campaign started off overtly Christian, acquiring its name from the concept of the Year of Jubilee in Leviticus. "Jubilee 2000" called for the "one-off cancellation of the unpayable debts of the world's poorest countries by the end of the year 2000, under a fair and transparent process." As the year 2000 passed, and more secular groups joined the effort, the campaign downplayed Jubilee in its name and rallied behind the slogan "Drop the Debt!" Governments and bankers resisted the demand but made some concessions, with strings attached. More recently there has been more commitment to dropping the debts, but campaigners complain it is still not enough.

So what's the beef? The contention is that poorer countries are under such a burden of debt that they spend more in debt repayments than on health and education. The argument goes that if their debt was cut these countries could spend much more on these vital areas, saving children's lives and giving the world's poor a new start. To boost their claims, the campaigners employ a few myths. Let's deal with the main two. First, rich

European nations allegedly made the poor nations poor through colonial exploitation and the appropriation of cheap raw materials and commodities. Second, in these poor nations the free market system purportedly benefited a colonial power elite to the detriment of the poor.

The first myth conveniently ignores the economic and administrative benefits colonialism gave to these nations. While there were abuses, the problem has to be put in perspective. This argument is built on the notion that the rich nations should feel guilty about the poor nations. However, many former colonies, such as America, Canada, Australia, New Zealand, Malaysia, and India, have hardly been exploited!

The second myth reveals the problem of state control and the corruption of power, rather than proving an innate weakness in the free market system. Corruption, bureaucracy, and price controls have stood in the way of poor people making money. The reality is that those with political power have kept the poor powerless and docile. Political decisions have superseded economic ones, thereby preventing economic growth. Positions of power have been filled through political patronage and bribery. Something needs to be done about poor economies, but the solution will never be purely economic, since political power and corruption play such a central part. Free enterprise actually favors the poor having power—"spending power." The free market system is built around expanding the middle class, not the lower class.

The theological evidence for this campaign is not convincing either. The texts in Leviticus apply to the land God gave to his people, the Israelites. There is no reference to land outside of Israel nor is the rule applied to those outside of the Jewish faith. Those called to observe the Jubilee were the Jewish people, and it was an observation directed at the Jewish "state." This was a common goal for a people with a common purpose.

The modern campaign is an imposition by organizations and individuals on other groups. The debt campaigners are applying their own interpretation of the Levitical rules to the whole world. They argue that God is the owner of all lands, so the rule applies to all lands. Yet this was never the understanding of the texts. What lies behind this debt manifesto is an assault on free enterprise through applying a different economic model. This is not about Jubilee but about a suspicion that the free market system is inherently wrong.

Is there not an element of self-righteousness in this campaign? Christian groups started the drive, but do they apply Leviticus to their own property dealings? These are organizations whose own transparency and finances need to be questioned, since many do not open their accounts publicly, which the banks and companies they attack are bound to do by law. We can ask why the rule applies to one component of the economy and not another. Indeed, there is more biblical support for the idea that the Christian groups should return land or offer remission of debts to their own tenants if Leviticus is to be followed. How can they expect the secular world to listen to an economic argument based on a biblical text if that argument is not applied to the economic dealings of those in the lobbying groups?

In recent years poverty campaigns have become nectar to celebrities, always with an eye on the media value. The Jubilee campaign is no exception, but should celebrities not ask more of themselves? They benefit from the free market system more than most because celebrity sells. Their business demands for high fees adds directly to the inflationary rise of global prices. Should they not question being remunerated for their efforts, which diverts funds away from community projects and education? Charity, as the saying goes, begins at home.

Campaigners have used many other biblical texts, apart from the core idea of Jubilee, to defend their policy option. One example comes earlier in Luke's Gospel where there is an echo of Jubilee in Jesus' reading from the scroll of Isaiah (Luke 4:16–21). We learn that Jesus is the one who has come "to proclaim the year of the Lord's favor." This is connected to the good news that is brought by Jesus to the poor. A text that does not get used is this one of the parable of the two debtors. Perhaps it is too theological, too spiritual a notion of debt cancellation. I suggest that this parable is passed over not because it is irrelevant to the issue, but because it is too inconvenient to the argument.

The context of the parable is Jesus' visit to the house of a Pharisee named Simon. A woman, we assume a prostitute, comes up to Jesus and washes his feet (with her tears), kisses him, and anoints him with perfume. These are usual acts that would be done for an honored guest, but Simon has not been so hospitable. This provokes the parable because the woman is overtaken by grief for the sins she has committed. The parable tells of two debtors who are forgiven vastly different amounts on the same terms. When asked, Simon rightly but grudgingly agrees that the one with the greater debt will be the more grateful for the cancellation of the debt.

This raises the question of whether forgiveness occurs proportionately. Jesus links the cancellation of the debt to the forgiveness of sins. The woman, who bears many sins, is more grateful for forgiveness than Simon, who we assume lives a more respectable life. The contrast is that the one who is forgiven little loves little, while the one who is forgiven much loves much. What has saved the woman is her faith, which erupts from her grief upon meeting the one who can truly forgive her sins— Jesus. Love and faith flow from the forgiveness of her many sins. Simon had assumed that the greater the sin, the harder the possibility for forgiveness. He judges that the woman's sins were so great that they were a total bar to relationship with God. The parable proves him wrong by showing that the forgiveness of great sins will be matched by great love.

But can we, should we, forgive at all? One could argue that forgiveness rests with God alone—it is never for us to forgive. We learn from the Lord's Prayer that we are to forgive (see Matthew 6:12; Luke 11:4). We can forgive by drawing an analogy from this prayer, and from this parable we learn that we ought to expect certain responses. We can take from this that we are to forgive others as we have been forgiven.

In Ephesians 4:32, Paul exhorts us: "Be kind and compassionate to one another, forgiving each other, just as in Christ God forgave you." Forgiveness is a negative action in the sense that our sins are wiped away. But it is also positive because in our forgiven state we find new life in Christ, who takes away the sins of the world. In Colossians 2:13 we read, "When you were dead in your sins and in the uncircumcision of your sinful nature, God made you alive with Christ. He forgave us all our sins." We learn that God can forgive the sins of any one of us and that we can (and must) forgive those whose sins are committed directly against us. But only God can actually forgive their sins. The quality of forgiveness is distinctly different.

We can wonder whether human forgiveness, distinct from divine forgiveness, has more to say about the symptoms than the causes of sin. Jesus firmly sets forgiveness in the context of our relationship with God. It is not a negotiation between people or nations, which is what debt relief amounts to. Our sinful nature is a corruption of what is God-given, and likewise corruption lies at the heart of the difficulties in poor nations. Economic corruption and warfare are rife in many of the poorest countries. My fear is that, while forgiveness of debt will wipe the slate clean, this will only create a tabula rasa for a new economic debacle.

The debt relief argument has two sides to it: the economic and the theological. As the campaign, originally initiated by Christian groups, became more secularized, so too was the theological side of the debate. Religious Jubilee became cancellation of debts (as I stated earlier, the cry changed from

"Jubilee 2000" to "Drop the Debt!") Debt cancellation has been taken up by certain politicians, seeking to push their own moral agenda. Whether debt forgiveness is a good economic policy is highly debatable. On face value, it seems like such a noble cause, but history is littered with good intentions. Realistically speaking, it has to be doubted that the policy works. The root causes of the economic problems remain untouched.

Poor countries need entrepreneurial activity to succeed. The solution to their economic problems are economic, along with a supportive political will. A convincing case can be made that wise stewardship of their economies will bring long-term solutions. I think people mistakenly believe that debt relief will go a long way to solving the problem, whereas what is in fact required is structural change of the economy accompanied by political reform. Many countries in Asia have taken this course and developed successful economies—without debt relief.

The main concern here, however, is not to examine the effectiveness or ineffectiveness of debt relief but to warn against theologizing the argument. We need to challenge the theological basis offered in this economic policy, as I suggest it is a distortion of the meaning of "forgiveness." Jesus does not offer us an international economic policy, nor does he call for Jubilee. He goes, rather, to the root of the human predicament: the need to be brought back into relationship with a forgiving God.

Certainly one stumbling block to our receiving God's forgiveness is our tendency to put other pursuits before

God. For the wealthy, this means that our wealth and comfort stand between us and true discipleship. The poor have an advantage in that they have little materially to get in the way; therefore, they tend to draw closer to God. The primary stumbling block for us all, however, is our lack of faith. It seems that instead of asserting Christ crucified for our sins there is often more confidence among Christians to support Christ the campaigner, Jesus the good moral example. But remember, in Luke's story the woman recognized Christ; Simon the Pharisee did not.

The fact is that the debt forgiveness campaign is a materialistic reading of the gospel. It needs to be rejected just as much as if a get-rich scheme based on a biblical work ethic were advanced as the meaning of the gospel. Biblical teaching is unequivocal in calling us to have concern for the poor and the hungry, but it is not a guidebook to economic policymaking. Debt relief will not solve the problem because it just resets the clock for corruption. Good economic management and less corruption are the ways in which the economic situation will change, which is why other developing nations, particularly in Asia, have been able to get themselves out of debt and create strong economies. (And the United States has greater debt than all the poor nations, so we could speculate about whether America will always remain wealthy!)

Like William Easterly, who wrote *The White Man's Burden: Why the West's Efforts to Aid the Rest Have Done So Much Ill and So Little Good* (Penguin, 2006), I feel a little po-faced (that's a British expression meaning "humorless and disapproving") in saying this, but the point is that the problem needs real solutions—not middle-class guilt or "the white man's burden." We are constantly thinking about how we can solve the problems of developing nations, rather than seeking to support them in solving their own problems by offering our expertise and by trading with them.

This is not to say there is no role for direct aid, nor that we are excused from giving. Our aid should be used to tackle the huge problems of drought and disease as well as sudden natural disasters, like the Christmas 2004 tsunami. Easterly asks the pertinent question of how Harry Potter books can get to all major stores in time for a midnight opening for the sake of the middle-class rich, but we can't get twelve-cent medicine to poor people. The good economics that achieve the former can also achieve the latter, so long as we encourage good economic practice and help cut out the disease of corruption in developing countries. Debt relief only deals with the symptoms; it won't keep the patient alive in the long term, even if it makes us feel better about ourselves.

I heartily recommend that you read Easterly's book if you want to explore these issues in depth, since this lies beyond my task in this book. My point is that we should not be seeking to biblically bless secular policies, especially when they do not solve the problem! The linking of biblical teaching in such a way undermines the real power of the gospel; it is advocacy without action, because it does not change the situation. The gospel has the power to change people's lives—people who in turn, on the basis of faith, will make real change happen in an uncertain economic world.

Other Biblical Texts to Study

Luke 7:41   Mark 6:37

Luke 7:42   Matthew 18:23–35; Ephesians 4:32;
Colossians 2:13–14

Luke 7:44   Genesis 18:1–4; 19:2; 43:24;
Judges 19:21; John 13:4–14;
1 Timothy 5:9–10

Luke 7:45   2 Samuel 15:5; Luke 22:47–48;
Romans 16:16

Luke 7:46   2 Samuel 12:20; Psalm 23:5;
Ecclesiastes 9:8; Daniel 10:3

Luke 7:48–49   Matthew 9:2–7; Mark 2:1–12;
Luke 5:18–26

Luke 7:50   Matthew 9:22; Mark 5:34;
Luke 8:48; 17:19; 18:42

Things to Think About

- Does forgiveness occur proportionately?

- Can we forgive others' sins? If so, how?

- Can we ask for or offer forgiveness on behalf of a previous generation? How do you decide what should be included?

- Do you agree that the debt forgiveness campaign is a materialistic reading of the gospel?

- Do you think debt cancellation will solve economic problems? If not, what alternatives will work?

- Why do you think Jesus talks about debt in the context of the woman's actions?

- Given the economic problems of the world, do you think Jesus should be a symbol for political campaign and protest?

CHAPTER 10

ARE WE STORING TREASURE ON EARTH?

The Parables of the Hidden Treasure and the Pearl

MATTHEW 13:44–46

Introduction

Jesus teaches us about the kingdom of heaven through the use of economic images. He tells us to get our priorities right. We are to seek the kingdom of God and not set store, or place our value, on our position in society or in our personal wealth.

In faith, we will be rewarded with the fruits of faith, which is the foundation for how we are to live in the economy.

The Parable

"The kingdom of heaven is like treasure hidden in a field. When a man found it, he hid it again, and then in his joy went and sold all he had and bought that field.

"Again, the kingdom of heaven is like a merchant looking for fine pearls. When he found one of great value, he went away and sold everything he had and bought it."

The Reflection

We all seek rewards in the economy. As we are seeking our personal reward, we can also glance sideways and see that some look like they're getting more out of the economy while others are losing out. The media screams out at the "fat cats," the leaders of corporations who are doing a lot better than we are. Strangely, we don't hear the same sustained attacks on sports stars and celebrities. There are vast sums involved in sports contracts, and top music stars and actors live lives beyond our wildest dreams. It seems that we demand accountability from leaders of companies that are generally listed on stock exchanges and are thus quite transparent, but we excuse, if not ooze over, the celebrities and sports stars whose accounts are not so disclosed.

Watching *Lifestyles of the Rich and Famous* can cause us to marvel at the opulence of people's homes and the luxury of their lives. It seems there are many treasures in the world; but when we look behind the walls of the rich houses, there is richness to be had by only a few. To this we hear the constant retort from protestors that this looks disgraceful in contrast to the excessive suffering of the poor in our own nation and around the world. The easy assumption to make is to suppose that we should limit what people get out of the economy. However, this immediately raises the question of how we decide who should get what and where we should draw the line.

The problem we can see here is that although we all get a piece of the economic pie, the size of the slices is very uneven. Like little Dickensian Olivers, we ask, "Please, sir, may I have some more?" Our share of the pie is measured by "profit," which is the reaping of dividends and money invested. There is a spectrum of wealth, from the "filthy rich" to the dying poor. This is the case across individual nations and across the world. Those opposing the free market system see this spectrum as the reason for condemning that system. Among them are Christians who see the goals of economic life as contrary to the good life of faith. The assumption at the heart of this view is that greed in the economy is the core problem in the world, driving a wedge between rich and poor.

This argument is a distraction for two reasons. First, the pursuit of profit is not the same thing as greed. In fact, the profit motive is the catalyst for growth in the economy. Yet greed and profit are frequently confused. Second, if we look at precapitalist economies, we can see there was greed back then as well. Greed in all its forms is part of humanity, including greed for money and power.

If one word sums up the whole moral disapproval of the free market system, it is this word *profit*. To defenders of the free market, the word describes an important and legitimate goal. It is a measure of success, for businesses need to make a profit for owners and employees alike. If a business cannot make a profit in the long term, it will go out of business. To opponents of free enterprise, the word is imbued with other meanings and is used as shorthand for greed and manipulation. This means businesses ruthlessly pursue profit to feed grasping shareholders, putting profit before all else.

It is hard to see how the free market system can operate without profit. It is equally hard to see how it can work in the way portrayed in the rhetoric of opponents. While some do pursue profit greedily, it is not intrinsic to wealth that it be pursued in that way. In addressing the economic ideas of antimarket "ethicists," we have to recall that decisions in the economy are not always rational. They are human decisions and so are often made on the criteria of ethical and public interest.

The fall of communism put to death any idea that the economy can be fully managed by the state. This is countered, however, by a belief that neither can the economy be left to freewheel through society—the upshot being that governments ponder how and when to apply the brakes. Those who argue against capitalism go astray because they assume the free market is a zero-sum game. They assume that if A buys from B, then A wins and B loses—or the other way around. Either way, someone has to lose! This is patently absurd. Since B has something A wants and has been able to pay for it by means of employment with C, have all parties not benefited? Now A has what he or she wants, B has the money, and C has the labor he or she needs. Everyone is happy.

We can look at this in context, if we want to assess the moral difficulties, but the problem is not the transaction as described. If the transaction involves the sale of a Bible, then we should feel quite happy about it. If the transaction involves a pornographic movie, then we would want to object. On this level we can have a full and frank moral debate. The issue is the moral nature of what is being purchased and the various folks involved, not the economic mechanism by which the transaction is achieved.

Profit still remains a major source of criticism and is regarded with much suspicion, but what exactly is it? On the simplest level, we can say profit is the subtraction of input from output, resulting in a surplus: in other words, the difference between what it cost to make a product and the price at which it is sold. This surplus is reinvested by wise firms in new product development as well as used to reward employees and improve the working environment. Clever businesses do these things knowing that happy workers are good workers. They also pay healthy dividends to investors to attract further investment.

We need to define what mechanisms of the free market are so objectionable to opponents of the market, such as socialists. Objectors essentially have difficulty in three areas: the role of markets, exchange production, and private ownership of capital. In the market economy, profits are derived from transactions related to private goods and services in exchange for money. The question arises as to whether individual transactions, such as the ones we just discussed, are morally dubious or if the combined set of transactions within the marketplace are morally dubious. This then gives rise to further objections, such as inequality of access to resources, resulting in what economists call "externalities" like ecological damage, dominance of monopolies over truly free markets, manipulation of individual wants, and a resultant consumerism and alienation in society.

At the heart of all these criticisms is a basic assumption that capitalism harnesses all that is bad in humanity for an aggregated result that benefits the rich and powerful, and that aggregated measure is profit. This drive for profit, critics say, is associated with greed, and together they form the "Baal" that is the free market economy. One supposes that if we were not greedy we would not need this "evil economy." To borrow from the Buddhist tradition, when a man points his finger at the moon, it is the fool who looks at the finger. Unfortunately, we see a lot of foolishness when it comes to moral assessments of the free market system.

Jesus warns us against foolishness in many of his parables and deals directly with our greed. In these two parables about treasure, Jesus is alluding to good stewardship. He talks about wealth and faith. By using these examples, Jesus shows that he does not see investment as wrong. Otherwise, would he not condemn the practice? Remember that in the parable of the talents the one who hoarded his wealth was condemned, for he had not invested wisely. Spiritually, we are not to hoard our faith either. Our faith is not something just for us, where we merely can know we are saved and bide our time until we meet our Lord. We are expected to do something with our faith. Our faith is to be developed and used in the world.

How, then, are we to do this with so many competing economic goals to be met? Doing our job, paying the bills, clothing our children, and other similar demands so often seem to take priority over our life of faith. Making a living, eking out an existence—such is the lot of humanity. From the beginning, since the banishment from God's garden of plenty, we have had to make use of the resources available on God's earth. This calls for self-reliance rather than dependency on others, and free enterprise thrives on such self-reliance. Added to this self-reliance are ingenuity and entrepreneurial activity, the desire to pursue something new in the world. These are the qualities that allow us to innovate the economy and make the best use of resources given to us by God.

A question arises as to how we value things in the economy. This is what the Greek philosopher Plato looked at with this water-diamond paradox. Why do we put such a low price on water, which is essential for life yet put such a high price on diamonds, which—beyond their industrial use—have little to commend them, even if they are "a girl's best friend"? Likewise, the "treasure" of which Jesus speaks. *Treasure* normally refers to gold, diamonds, and jewels, all things of little practical value. The pearl of which Jesus speaks is a mere bauble. Yet Jesus takes these things that people have treasured for centuries, long before Tiffany's put a price on them, and compares them to finding our Lord and coming to know the kingdom of God.

These two little parables put the real contrast before us. They show us the *real* treasures to be found, treasures that can't be bought in any store! Those who place their sense of worth in the things of this world, who build themselves up in comfort apart from faith, are storing up treasures on earth. As the old saying goes, you can't take it with you! Yet what we treasure is not necessarily extravagant pearls and baubles; we can set our hearts on many small treasures, material things or other desires that we put before God. We can find ourselves pulled toward covetousness of the things of this world instead of focusing on the "world" the Lord promises us: the kingdom of heaven.

When we set a political agenda at the heart of our understanding of the gospel, we are also setting our hearts on the treasures of this world. This is because we are seeing the material realm as a solution to the ultimate gift that is the gospel. We can covet political promises just as much as the things of wealth. If we do that, then we become materialistic, not just in the sense of consumerism or wealth but also in our understanding of the antidote: the Word that became flesh, that came into the world born of a virgin, only to die a criminal's death, yet triumphed in the resurrection and the promise of everlasting life.

All of these teachings become devalued when we turn to a material gospel. These doctrines are then judged to be of lesser importance than the teachings of "justice and peace," the social gospel that is at the heart of secular salvation. The Lord whom we worship, the kingdom of God that we seek, is no longer held up as the hidden treasure or the shining pearl. Secular and social policy goals are coveted instead. Neglecting these points of doctrine, traditional churches are being torn apart by joyless arguments over economic inequality, human rights, gay rights, international conflicts, and any number of other things.

These parables take us back to the joy that is central to doctrine, the belief that Jesus invites us all into the kingdom of heaven. We are not to covet the things of this world but to take his gospel to the world—a world where so many pursue wealth and power, baubles and influence. These "treasures" fade in the light of the salvation that is freely offered and can be joyfully embraced in this world. If we seek his kingdom first, then we will find our reward in the here and now by living in the joy of faith; and we can also grasp that there is a place prepared for us in the kingdom to come. Storing treasure on earth will gain us neither.

The secret of these two brief parables is that they were spoken by Jesus together; they form a contrasting pair. The hidden treasure tells of a joy like that of the disciples who find their Lord. The merchant in search of fine pearls is in a different situation: he sells all to buy the pearl of great value. Why is the pearl so precious? Why is the kingdom of God like a pearl or like treasure hidden in a field?

Jesus is offering us a paradox, one that sets how we treasure things in the world against the need to find our Lord and seek his kingdom. These things we treasure are insignificant compared to his Word. Whatever we treasure in the economy is impoverished by his Word. If we get lost in envy, materialism, greed, and the pursuit of treasure in this world, then we will be lost. We are called to watchfulness, which means being aware at all times that God is watching over us. We are to be ready in joy for his call.

Other Biblical Texts to Study

Matthew 13:44	Isaiah 55:1–3a; Matthew 13:24
Matthew 13:45	Philippians 3:7–11

Things to Think About

- How should we react to the wealth of other people?

- Do you think redistribution is a realistic option to the reality of uneven slices of the economic pie?

- Do you agree with those who contend that greed is the core problem in the world today?

- What do you think stewardship means for you today?

- Is it enough to call others to faith, or are we also responsible to address the economic situation of others—both rich and poor?

- Has God provided enough for all of us? If so, why is there scarcity in the economy?

- Why do you think Jesus uses treasures to communicate about the kingdom of God?

CHAPTER 11

How Much Do We Give?

The Parable of the Pharisee and the Tax Collector

LUKE 18:9–14

Introduction

Jesus often used the Pharisees as an example. Their approach is opposite to the everyday appeal of the parables. This parable asks us to examine our pride. It also raises the question of giving and whether doing all the "right" things is what makes us better people. We abdicate our responsibility to others when we feel we are above others and have overcome our sinful nature.

The Parable

To some who were confident of their own righteousness and looked down on everybody else, Jesus told this parable: "Two men went up to the temple to pray, one a Pharisee and the other a tax collector. The Pharisee stood up and prayed about himself: 'God, I thank you that I am not like other men—robbers, evildoers, adulterers—or even like this tax collector. I fast twice a week and give a tenth of all I get.'

"But the tax collector stood at a distance. He would not even look up to heaven, but beat his breast and said, 'God, have mercy on me, a sinner.'

"I tell you that this man, rather than the other, went home justified before God. For everyone who exalts himself will be humbled, and he who humbles himself will be exalted."

The Reflection

Augustine suggested that government is merely an act of piracy on a grand scale. He asked, "Justice being taken away, then, what are kingdoms but great robberies? For what are robberies themselves, but little kingdoms?" To theologians and church leaders wishing to hitch the gospel to a political agenda, this must sound like the ultimate heresy by the early father. It has become almost an article of faith that welfare and entitlement programs are the means to achieve the Good Society. Thus it is no longer considered correct to think the individual needs to be transformed. It is a little ironic that the state, which put Jesus to death, is seen as the focus of good in our lives.

Believing they will only be listened to when they approve of the secular agenda, church leaders have learned to ape the elites of secular society. They should have more confidence in the gospel. They ought to voice the ageless views of faith and correct the social mores of the day. There is a tendency among the elites of society to show how good they are. They want to ensure they make everyone aware of their position, and yours. They look down at those working in commerce—the managers, tradesmen, and storekeepers. They secretly pray, "God, I thank you that I am not like other people: traders, CEOs, capitalists, or even like this chartered accountant!" In a modern retelling of this parable we might hear about the tax collector being exalted as part of the machinery of government, then it falls to the chartered accountant or entrepreneur to be the lowly figure to beg forgiveness.

In this parable Jesus points to the contrast between those who exalt their deeds and those who are humbled by their inadequacy before God. He uses the example of the pious Pharisee and the lowly tax collector. As so often with Jesus, the figure of approval is the one whom we can least admire. The tax collector knows he has done great wrongs. In this knowledge he lowers his head, beats his breast, and pleads for God's mercy.

The Pharisee, meanwhile, stands tall in his piety, telling God how good he is at keeping the faith.

How often we see this pharisaic behavior on our televisions as people tell us how right their actions are and inform us of how we can build a better tomorrow. Humanity is exalted in this moment, and the people stand tall at how we can deliver ourselves. Again we meet one of Jesus' great reversals. For the exalted shall be humbled: the plans of mice and men! How often do we see the great and the good of our society admit to their mistakes or humble themselves as people who are short of God's demands? Jesus tells us of his reversal: The humble shall be exalted.

Those who delight in the praise of their actions, who do good to feel good, will only be exalted in their own eyes and perhaps the eyes of other people, but not before God. Before God, they shall be humbled. This is a text that betrays any idea that we can be saved by our own merit. We cannot work our way to a place at the Lord's table. Those who tread such a path have taken the wrong route. If we want to take the right route, we have to be like the tax collector: humbling ourselves to face God's judgment. Then we shall receive the greatest recognition of all, the gift of grace given to us by God. Like the tax collector, we can then have our prayers answered, our plea accepted. Only then can we take the right path, the one that carries us home to our Lord. As the humbled, we shall be exalted.

The elites of our society are the Pharisees of our modern economy. They "know" what is best for everyone else: "If only you could see it, if only you could believe that all of society can be planned!" Yet can we not say that welfarism has been, in the long term, destructive in its effects on people's lives? It has taught us to abdicate care and responsibility. It leaves the state to sort out the problems around us, even our own family problems: put Grandma in a home, abort Jenny's teenage pregnancy, have Uncle John arrested for abuse. The state will take control of these problems, marginalizing the role of family in the process. This causes the institution of the family to decline in significance as the state and new patterns of family create a new norm. "Care" has become a professional activity, rather than the thoughtful attitude and response of individuals and families.

In modern times, the state has become the instrument of social engineering. The state is in a battle against the "anarchy" of the free market, which can only do good under the benevolent oversight of the state. Perhaps the unfortunate truth is that pragmatic economics and free markets are the most effective because they are based on what we are like. If we function out of rampant consumerism, then this is reflected in the economy. The economy is merely a measure of how self-absorbed we really are, holding up a mirror to our modern civilization and revealing its vanity. We could point to the Genesis narrative and suggest there is an economic effect of original sin, which stops us from enjoying the Planner's garden of Eden and banishes us to the harsh realities of the economic pursuit of gain. Thus we live in the "solitary, poor, nasty, brutish, and short" state of existence warned of by the seventeenth-century British philosopher Thomas Hobbes.

This much is clear: we need some boundaries for how we organize ourselves economically. The question this poses, however, is to what extent should we use rules, self-regulation, and government to ensure that we all play the economic game fairly. The failure of communism was that the state could not manage the economy. We can legitimately challenge the extent to which the state, in our mixed economies of private enterprise and public administration, should be involved in management of the economy. How big should government be? How much do we need to be governed? These are legitimate questions.

Harvard philosopher Robert Nozick asked the question: If the state did not exist, would it be necessary to invent it? The outcome of any such debate is always likely to be affirmative, but there would be wildly divergent views as to what should constitute the necessary state. This is quite apart from the state we have or the state the government of the day would like it to be. This is evident in the discussion over what the economic role of the state should be and to what extent government should move toward attempting to manage the economy rather than leaving things to the market.

When we see the extent to which governments legislate our economic activities, often under the guise of public interest, we might be inclined to identify with the "inconveniences" of the state outlined, in almost biblical language, in an attack on state interference by the French economist Pierre-Joseph Proudhon. His invective against state influence over us is partly informed by a sense that the state is not necessarily the focus of all hope and that perhaps other mechanisms, such as the market, can also deliver hope.

Government apparatus can often be bedeviled by bureaucracy, ineptness, and sheer indifference to those whom they are set up to serve. These bureaucratic servants can treat their "customers" with the superior disdain of knowing that the state they are working for, unlike a private business, won't go under and that their jobs are considerably safer than those in the private sector. That aside, it is questionable that the state apparatus is sensitive to the needs and choices of the people it pretends to serve. Such state bodies can demonstrate great versatility in their arguments for planning, only to find public dissatisfaction with their grand designs.

On the other hand, the marketplace can achieve better results without such a belief in design, preferring to leave the mutual interests of market participants to achieve the desired end. This is the idea suggested by Adam Smith's explanation of the "invisible hand" operating in the marketplace.

Against such an argument one can naturally expect the welfarist to point to the failures in the free market system and advocate that the state has a higher moral purpose than do market participants. Again, we find the Jekyll and Hyde argument that people behave differently in business than at home, though in the state official we are led to believe that we have a Jekyll and Jekyll character. Those who contend that government should manage the economic state of affairs have redistribution of wealth at the heart of their economic understanding. The argument goes that every state must accept at least a minimal welfare role in its function. If we reduce the state to a protective functionary, this still implies that there is some sense in which the state is involved in helping out others. This rationale is then extended to the economic sphere on the basis that the state can also help others by redistribution of economic resources.

Nozick raises a further point, one that is at the heart of the anti-globalization mentality: there is a body of opinion that doesn't like the market outcome, what Nozick called "a mutually reinforcing process," and they want to dictate outcomes or be the arbiters of taste on such matters as the quality of burgers to the use of pesticides. Yet, as purchasers of fashionable labels and cheap airline tickets, they have been more than willing to exchange. In this mutually reinforcing process, these designer protestors have become themselves part of the market. Their message is one that sells to the disaffected offspring of the baby boomers, a kind of Club Med for malcontents. They are part of what makes the market tick because all values have become "marketable," even those of protest, a point that also explains the popularity of the repackaged and well-marketed "New Labour" brand in Britain, a kind of Democrat-Lite.

Thus, those who hold the "right views," read the "right newspapers," and do the "right thing" do so as they look down on those who are "wrong" and lesser than themselves. Their aim is to create the "right society" or the "Good Society." We saw an example of this attitude in the 2004 U.S. presidential election as the elite mocked "ignorant" red states, or "Jesus states," which voted for President Bush: "Such ignorance must have something to do with religion in these states because faith is ignorance, isn't it?" "Thank God," they prayed, "that we are enlightened, unlike these people of faith."

We see the same attitude in the economy. Free enterprise works best when individuals pursue their self-interest; but this needs to be limited somehow, and the elite want to police this limitation. The gospel calls us as believers to limit ourselves, and we are to define our self-interest in terms of faith. This means we should not lie, cheat, or deceive—all of the things that disrupt a well-oiled market mechanism. This sort of corruption is what typically lies at the heart of many of the economic failures in developing countries and also, closer to home, corporate failures. It also lies at the heart of poor government. (Remember Augustine?)

Like Plato's *Republic* and Marx's *Internationale*, the elite seek to change the economic world through the use of social engineering. Economic progress has become the modern religion. By organizing society in a particular way, people develop confidence that secular salvation can be achieved. The nongovernmental organizations (NGOs), or civil society groups as they call themselves, are the new acolytes. Churches are transformed into "peace and justice centers" or "ethically acceptable (in whose view?) marketplaces." "Thank God," they pray, "that we know what the solution is to the myriad of economic and political questions."

This is about people searching for economic religion. Having lost faith in Marxism, socialism, and other failed ideologies, many have now turned to environmental fundamentalism and human rights advocacy to express their humanism. "Thank God," they pray, "that we know what is good for the environment a hundred years from now and what rights need to be protected over others." There is a judgmental aspect that appears and that denies others who disagree with this approach. Conservatives are to be engaged in "fair debate," which means as long as they eventually accept these progressive rights and economic ideas.

Pharisaism is alive and well in modern America and across the world. This prayer of not being like others is mouthed by many. The humility of the gospel is lost in the human ego as it seeks to promote the Good Society. The state can tell us what to do and show us how to behave. Yet what of the individual? What of freedom? The prayer we are called to express is the acknowledgment of our wretchedness before God, an act of humility. Only then can we stand tall. The elites of our modern society who pray "Thank God we are not like people of simple faith" may feel they can stand up tall, but they will always be— to use a phrase from Alexis de Tocqueville—"haunted by visions of what will be."

Other Biblical Texts to Study

Luke 18:9	Isaiah 65:5; Luke 16:14–15; Romans 14:3–4, 10
Luke 18:10	2 Kings 20:5, 8; Acts 3:1
Luke 18:11	Matthew 6:5; Mark 11:25; Luke 22:40
Luke 18:12	Isaiah 58:3; Matthew 9:14; Luke 11:42
Luke 18:13	Ezra 9:6; Isaiah 66:2; Jeremiah 31:19; Luke 5:27–32; 23:48; 1 Timothy 1:15
Luke 18:14	Matthew 23:12; Luke 14:11

Things to Think About

- Is Augustine fair in saying government is like piracy?

- Do you believe that government is the good that can create a better society?

- What do you think the role of the state is, and how does the individual fit in?

- Is there a division between the elite and those of simple faith?

- Has "welfarism" and big government taught us to abdicate our individual responsibilities?

- While we cannot build a utopia, can we strive for the Good Society as the best and most fair society possible? How should this be achieved?

- Do you agree that pharisaism is alive and well in the world today?

CHAPTER 12

WHAT CAN WE DO TO HELP OTHERS?

The Rich Man and Lazarus

LUKE 16:19–31

Introduction

It is easy for us to live well and build a cocoon of faith and wealth, leaving those outside of faith and outside of wealth to fend for themselves. In this parable, Jesus warns us against such an attitude, lest we become like the rich man and ignore the plight of the less fortunate.

The Parable

"There was a rich man who was dressed in purple and fine linen and lived in luxury every day. At his gate was laid a beggar named Lazarus, covered with sores and longing to eat what fell from the rich man's table. Even the dogs came and licked his sores.

"The time came when the beggar died and the angels carried him to Abraham's side. The rich man also died and was buried. In hell, where he was in torment, he looked up and saw Abraham far away, with Lazarus by his side. So he called to him, 'Father Abraham, have pity on me and send Lazarus to dip the tip of his finger in water and cool my tongue, because I am in agony in this fire.'

"But Abraham replied, 'Son, remember that in your lifetime you received your good things, while Lazarus received bad things, but now he is comforted here and you are in agony. And besides all this, between us and you a great chasm has been fixed, so that those who want to go from here to you cannot, nor can anyone cross over from there to us.'

"He answered, 'Then I beg you, father, send Lazarus to my father's house, for I have five brothers. Let him warn them, so that they will not also come to this place of torment.'

"Abraham replied, 'They have Moses and the Prophets; let them listen to them.'

"'No, father Abraham,' he said, 'but if someone from the dead goes to them, they will repent.'

"He said to him, 'If they do not listen to Moses and the Prophets, they will not be convinced even if someone rises from the dead.'"

The Reflection

We have often stopped along the path that these parables have taken us to consider what "a rich man" is in reality. In the time of Jesus the rich were a small minority indeed, and the poor were all around. Today's economy is quite different, since in the West the vast majority of us are comparatively rich—even if we don't always feel that way! Despite widespread poverty in the less developed countries, there are many who are rich, and there is great potential for increased wealth.

Much of Europe, including the leading capitalist economy of Britain, once had poverty like that of today's lesser developed economies. Today, because economic wealth can be achieved by good economic management, these poor nations themselves have greater possibilities for their tomorrow. Yet it seems so often that state planning or political will are supposed to triumph while commerce is denied its role as the driver of economic success. This is a little like asking your medical doctor to unclog your sink. Perhaps he can do it, but he doesn't have professional skills to offer in this area. Likewise, good economics and commercial management are the way to create economic wealth. Political will can help by not hindering commerce and by not putting red tape and bureaucracy in the way of people trying to be entrepreneurial. Political will in these countries can also help by stamping out corruption in their dealings.

When we see poverty in our communities or elsewhere in the world, we cannot help but contrast this with our own wealth. However, we can also look up the social scale and feel our own lack of wealth compared to others. Perhaps we can sometimes feel that little tinge of envy. If we do not appreciate how wealthy we are in reality, then we feel we ought to have more. To a greater or lesser extent, there is a little envy in all of us. Wealth and poverty touches our feelings in different ways. If we help the poor, then we can feel good about ourselves and feel empowered in some way, perhaps unaware of the sense that the poor have in fact become an object to us. This is not to sound cynical about all our actions; it is to point out that there is an element of these unwanted feelings within us, whether we like it or not.

There was no such struggle in the heart of the rich man in our parable, since he was completely disinterested in the poor man. (I will note here that some Bible interpreters have questioned if this passage truly is a parable. Such issues aren't germane to this book, but suffice it to say that I certainly take this to be a parable.) Oddly, the poor man, Lazarus, is the only character given a name in any of the parables in the New Testament. Lazarus may recall the servant of Abraham in Genesis. The rich man here is sometimes called Dives, which is Latin for "rich man." The two men in the parable are vividly contrasted. The rich man lives only for himself, lavishing luxury on himself—as evidenced by the wearing of purple, the color associated with great wealth. The poor man is excluded, outside of the gates, and is plagued by sores and hungry for whatever scraps may fall from the rich man's table. The religious or moral status of the two men is not provided to us; we are called to ask the question, to use our judgment as to what difference may be understood. In verses 22–26, we learn to what end the two men come.

There is then a twist to the parable, for the rich man is told that his brothers have Moses and the Prophets to appeal to if they want to avoid the rich man's plight. The problem for the rich man is not caused by his wealth but by his ignorance of the teachings of Scripture. He distanced himself from God and thought his riches adequate to satiate his needs in the world. The mention of Abraham underlines the point because Abraham himself was rich yet is one of the great fathers of the faith, for he subordinated all else in his service to God. In hell the rich man learns his fate and finds his condemnation. His response is finally to look to his neighbor and warn his brothers, but this comes too late to save him.

The audience to which this parable is directed is once again the Pharisees, reaching back to verses 14–15. Jesus is telling them a story about what awaits those wedded to this life and that the good fortunes of the rich in this life will be reversed in the next, with a warning to the rich against being covetous. We too are being given a message about what can greet us in the world beyond this one. This is a solemn parable that warns us of the reversal of fortunes that may await us. It also draws the conclusion that if the Law and the Prophets cannot change the hearts of those wedded to this world, then a miracle such as the resurrection will not succeed either. We are to root our faith in the resurrection if we are to avoid the condemnation that greeted the rich man.

However, we also have to look at the full implication of this parable as one that says something about our responsibility to others. Had the problem of wealth been just about the attitude of the rich man, then there was no need to include Lazarus in the story. All Jesus would have had to say was that the rich man lived lavishly and selfishly and then paid for it in hell. Why include Lazarus? Jesus is warning us that we have to view ourselves, as part of the broader community, in relation to others. We cannot selfishly imagine that we alone stand before God, devoid of how we have responded to the needs of others. The real contrast is between choosing to serve God with our money and using money idolatrously to secure our final condemnation in the Lord's courts.

The rich man is condemned because he loved wealth and declined to help the poor man at his gate, not even with crumbs from his table. To underline the distance between the rich man and Lazarus, we are told even the dogs took sympathy on the poor man by licking his sores. The rich man has eschewed his responsibilities toward the poor man who has come seeking his help. He is so self-absorbed that he probably doesn't even consider the plight of the wretched man at his gate.

This raises questions about how we "gate" ourselves in communities today, keeping ourselves distanced from the woes of many in places close to us as well as around the world. By changing the channel to something more cheerful, the TV remote allows us to regulate how much misery we wish to witness. When we see a beggar in the street, it is easy to throw him a few cents to appease our conscience. We too can often behave like the rich man, ignoring the plight of the one who seeks help at our "gate." In many cases, concern for those outside the gates is seen as a job for the government or the police. The Christian response needs to be one of discipleship, offering our faith, prayers, and help to those without faith and in need of prayer and help.

In reaching out to the people around us and those in faraway places, we need to understand the totality of the power within us and our church community. This is not just about money and assisting the poor. It is also about prayer, education, and sustaining a vibrant congregation. It is about building our own faith community to be powerful in prayer and ministry. It is about calling others and welcoming newcomers into our community so that we increase our strength as God's people. To see this only in terms of dollars and cents is to miss the unique mission of the church, which is distinct from all the secular agencies that exist to help the community. The church needs to stand as an exemplar in the community and also as a negotiator between various community actors, in order to help people help themselves.

In the frustration of seeing the plight of the poor, it is easy to think there is a political response that can be bound to a theological concern. There is then a risk in taking a particular political view of the economic woes that afflict people at home and abroad. Once the churches or Christian groups politicize this role and advocate policy, then they run the risk of alienating themselves from the community and becoming indistinguishable from any other provider of help. The role of negotiator will then be diminished and the status of exemplar weakened.

Both the church and individual Christians have roles to play. As an individual Christian, you should participate in the policy debates about how to best change your community. You will no doubt find yourself on the opposite side of the aisle from other Christians on many issues. This is healthy because you are dealing with the fallible nature of humanity and the difficulty of weighing all the different possibilities. At the end of a debate about policy options, you and your opponent should be able to kneel in prayer, together facing God in humility and in need of guidance. The danger is when churches or Christian groups become advocates of policy, alienating the opposition by following the narrow interests of political groups and passing fashion. Christ's gospel is timeless and counter to culture, but public policy is within history and tied to the limited vision of human culture. The question is where you want to place your confidence.

Jesus invites us to consider what we place our confidence in and how we act in community with others. We are to assess whether we feel so secure in our faith, so secure in our personal wealth, that we have made ourselves quietly independent of the world and its troubles. Our faith and our wealth is to be used in community with others. In terms of wealth, this does not mean that we give all our money away and become poor ourselves. Using our wealth can mean many things, for we are rich in many things. Because we live well, we have a greater capacity to help; and there is a variety of ways we can help this missionary work of the church.

We ought to examine ourselves and discern whether we are really doing all we can to help the church and the community toward achieving better things. We may have skills that can be put to good use for the church or in pro bono work. We may hold a position in our work where we can make a difference in people's lives by encouraging the decision makers to do things for the good. We might have daily interaction with people in the stores or on the street where we might be able to do something to make their lot more sustainable.

Of course, we need to sustain ourselves. We can't be of much use to someone else if we cannot help ourselves. The key is to recognize when we are able to help and to know what we have within our power to change. The old saying that charity begins at home does have some validity, for it means that we have to help from a position of strength—in our faith and in our material being. Ultimately, what makes anyone's lot sustainable is the gift of God's grace.

Our self-examination is not posed here as a condemnation but as a challenge to see whether we maximize who and what we are to the greater glory of God. It is for each of us, not a focus group or a government policy, to answer this question. Nor is this an occasion for finger-wagging. The fate that awaits us at the end times, should we ignore such self-examination and submission to his will, is made painfully clear in this parable.

Other Biblical Texts to Study

Luke 16:20   Acts 3:2

Luke 16:21   Matthew 15:21–28

Luke 16:22   Luke 19:9–10

Luke 16:23   Matthew 11:23–24

Luke 16:24   Matthew 25:41–46; Luke 3:8

Luke 16:25   Luke 6:20–26

Luke 16:28   Acts 2:40

Luke 16:29   Luke 4:17–19; Luke 24:27, 44;
                John 1:45; 5:45–47; Acts 15:21

Things to Think About

* Do you think economic problems can best be solved
  by good economics and commercial management or by
  government planning?

* What do you see as the best balance between totally
  free enterprise and government intervention?

* In what ways can you practically help those less
  fortunate in faith or wealth?

* If you work for a business, does it support many
  community projects? Could your company do more? If
  so, who do you need to talk to about this?

- Do you feel that we cut ourselves off and create "gated" communities—that is, set apart from the problems of other communities?

- Do we rely too much on government and the police to resolve social problems? Are these problems too big for individuals and communities to sort out for themselves?

- What more can be done in your church and community to reach out to help others?

- Do you agree that "charity begins at home," meaning that we need to be strong first ourselves before we can help others? Is this idea too simplistic? If so, what alternative would you suggest?

CHAPTER 13

HOW CHARITABLE ARE WE?

The Parable of the Great Banquet

LUKE 14:15–24

― ⌒ ―

Introduction

Do we take for granted our place at the great banquet the Lord is providing for us? And what are we to make of those who decline his invitation? This parable provides us with the hope that there is a place prepared for us, but it also warns those who refuse Christ. The parable also raises questions about the role of charity and how we are to be charitable to those less fortunate than us.

The Parable

When one of those at the table with him heard this, he said to Jesus, "Blessed is the man who will eat at the feast in the kingdom of God."

Jesus replied: "A certain man was preparing a great banquet and invited many guests. At the time of the banquet he sent his servant to tell those who had been invited, 'Come, for everything is now ready.'

"But they all alike began to make excuses. The first said, 'I have just bought a field, and I must go and see it. Please excuse me.'

"Another said, 'I have just bought five yoke of oxen, and I'm on my way to try them out. Please excuse me.'

"Still another said, 'I just got married, so I can't come.'

"The servant came back and reported this to his master. Then the owner of the house became angry and ordered his servant, 'Go out quickly into the streets and alleys of the town and bring in the poor, the crippled, the blind and the lame.'

"'Sir,' the servant said, 'what you ordered has been done, but there is still room.'

"Then the master told his servant, 'Go out to the roads and country lanes and make them come in, so that my house will be full. I tell you, not one of those men who were invited will get a taste of my banquet.'"

The Reflection

In "the City" in London, England's Wall Street, there is an old saying, "My word is my bond," which indicates that trust and knowing who you are doing business with is core to how the world of finance should work. In that same financial district, there is an annual banquet held in the grand Mansion House, where the key speaker is the British finance minister—a time when politics and finance rub shoulders for an evening. Every day in the City and on Wall Street, business lunches are held to seal a business deal or woo a journalist. Meals are important. We read in the society pages of newspapers and in glossy magazines about big charity dinners; and we have fundraising dinners in our local churches. Dinners are set out for thousands of dollars or just a few dollars, allowing people to mix their social life with giving to charitable causes. There are any number of reasons to "break bread."

The Lord's Supper is core to the life of the church, whether it is practiced every Sunday, once a month, or once a quarter. The Supper takes us back to the Lord's last times with the disciples. Knowing that he will leave them, he chooses to break bread with them and explain what must be done after his death. This is the meal we are to take with the Lord until the great banquet; and in our parable the terms of entry to that banquet are set before us. To this banquet all are invited, especially those who are more likely to be the recipients of funds raised by charity dinners than those with their knives and forks poised. Anyone who has arranged even a small dinner party or social event knows the nerves it causes before the guests arrive, wondering if all the good work will go to waste. In this story, that is exactly what happens!

Many people are invited to the banquet in the parable, and initially they accept; but when the final invitations are presented, they have other priorities and so provide nothing but excuses— and not even good ones at that! One says he needs to inspect some land he has bought, but do you think he would have bought such land without seeing it first? A second says he has bought five yoke of oxen, but how many farmers or landowners would buy so much stock unseen? The third one is a little different, saying that he cannot come because he has just gotten married. This excuse takes us back to an Old Testament exemption from military service (Deuteronomy 20:7; 24:5), but does this apply to a generous invitation to a feast? These are excuses that are tied to love of possessions and family and are to be put aside in our love of God.

The response of the host to these excuses is understandably one of anger, so he invites the poor and the needy to his table until all the seats are taken. This has often been interpreted as a warning to pious Jews who reject the gospel, but it is unlikely that Jesus would only invite the poor once he himself has been rejected by the pious. Instead our attention is to be focused on the host, who is prepared to invite all to his table even though some will not accept the invitation. The image of the host in the parable sitting with the poor and needy readily brings to mind Jesus and his willingness to break bread with tax collectors and sinners. The great banquet that Jesus invites us to will not be filled with all of high society, important people in public life and celebrities, but those sinners who have accepted his invitation. Again, Jesus reverses the social order of this life and reminds us that all we achieve or have in this life is as nought if we do not accept his invitation now. This offer is given to all, but it also contains a warning to those who refuse. To be blessed in our life ahead and the life to come depends upon our acceptance here and now.

When we look around us and at what we have, our possessions count as nothing before his open arms. We stand alone before him; and everything has been done for us. We cannot work our way to the table, nor can we pay for our seat at the banquet. Jesus has made this all possible for us: the price has been paid by his going to the cross, a greater price than any of us is capable of paying. In the face of such an invitation, how can we refuse? Yet many, complacent in their own comfort and thought, do just that. Just as the invitation to dine is to us alone, so too will the one who refuses the invitation dine alone on the day of judgment. Jesus spells this out clearly, saying that those who refuse shall not get a taste of his banquet. When we accept his invitation, when we know in our hour of crisis what must be done, then we walk in his ways and work as his disciples.

We should recall this parable when we undertake charitable work and ask ourselves why we do it and what part it plays in our discipleship. The wealthy philanthropist with his or her foundation and the wealthy individual who buys tickets for a charity dinner or ball are trading in good favor. They provide the funds while gaining the prestige of a foundation in their name or getting their profile in a glossy magazine for all their friends to see. Perhaps this is a cynical way of looking at what they are doing; and we should recognize that people can enjoy themselves while doing good for the less fortunate. Even in the parable, can we not argue that the host only invited the poor out of anger at being snubbed by his social equals? Charity has always been at the heart of the Christian way of life and is called for in its own right. Responding to God, rather than to have a good time or to raise our profile, is the reason for doing good. If the latter are our reasons, then all we are doing is carrying out a materialist function of trading our goodwill for something in return. Charity then becomes a transaction much like any other. This also raises questions for the hosts of such charity events because they are making a transaction of giving something in return, knowing that people will only give to their cause if they make it in their interest to attend.

As so often with Jesus, this raises difficult questions about our motivation for doing good things. At best, our motives should be borne out of our love of God: doing good for the love of God. If we have wealth, we give money to help the poor.

If we do not (or even if we do), then we can volunteer at a charity event or work a night at a soup kitchen, which costs us nothing but our time. At worst, our motives can be borne out of self-grandeur. If we have wealth and we demand something in return, namely some recognition, or if we do good out of guilt, then we give nothing of ourselves in reality. Being human, our motives are most probably mixed. This does not exclude the possibility of enjoying ourselves while helping others, indeed the gospel suggests that we should enjoy our service to God and others. However, the question of motive still remains to be examined—which is exactly what this parable challenges us to do.

How often are we really charitable in our lives? An act of charity can be directed at anyone who needs our help, whether that person asks for it or not. In the parable, the people who attend the banquet in the end did not ask to be invited; a generous offer was made to them. In one of our other parables, the parable of the rich man and Lazarus, poor Lazarus is waiting at the gate for the crumbs that fell from the rich man's table. In both parables, Jesus shows us the breadth of how we might act: from generously offering an open invitation to responding to a specific cry for help.

The expectation on our side regarding the charity we offer is that we expect those we help to help themselves if they can or to seek the help they need. The idea of charity is generally one of limited help: providing assistance in order for people in need to help themselves, if they are able to do so. There are those who can never help themselves, who need constant support from charitable sources and will sadly perhaps never become independent of this help. However, there are others who could help themselves, if only they had the capital and tools for the task. Providing this kind of support is the most effective, for it restores human dignity to people and leaves them independent and free to pursue life as they wish. Such individuals do not remain beholden; they get out of trouble and move on. This kind of support also makes the recipients accountable because they need to act in ways that will at a later date return the capital or help offered.

Free enterprise allows those with a little capital and the right tools to help themselves and then to help others. Though the trick is to get started, there is a growing trend in poverty support to encourage this approach. This has started to move people from dependence to independence. What better charity can there be than that? This also leaves charities to help those who need it most: the poor who are too poor to help themselves and the crippled, blind, and lame who cannot help themselves because of physical incapacity. We can make this distinction, recognizing what form of help is most needed and ensuring that those who can help themselves are able to make progress as rapidly as possible. Policies that keep them dependent are of little help to them or to those who pay their way.

We have to accept the fact that, in reality, there are many people on the edges of our society who are capable of leading dignified lives yet choose to live on the edges. There were such people in the time of Jesus, and there are still such people today. They cannot be made the scapegoat for uncharitable attitudes.

Helping people in this situation requires spiritual change: a change in the way they live and understand themselves. God has made us in his own image; and this is why we are to have dignity for ourselves—in order to honor him. We are to do all we can to reach out and help people restore this dignity. But here too many people will refuse to come to his table. Rejection of his invitation is not just a prerogative of the rich.

For all its weaknesses, the market economy does offer freedom to pursue work and to choose how we spend our money, including supporting ourselves in order to do works of service for the church and for others. It also, alas, provides freedom for those who have different wants and goals. Other forms of organized economies do not guarantee as much freedom as market economies consistently have, and as yet there is no imagined alternative to the system we have that could succeed more. As we have speculated elsewhere in this book, the only way we could have a "Christian economy" is by filling the world with Christians first, for otherwise we would be forcing a worldview on others as to how they should live economically. Jesus never coerced; he only asked. We always have the option to refuse his invitation—and to dine elsewhere.

Other Biblical Texts to Study

Luke 14:15	Isaiah 25:6; Matthew 26:29; Revelation 19:9
Luke 14:16	Matthew 22:1–14
Luke 14:20	Deuteronomy 20:7; 24:5; 1 Corinthians 7:32–35
Luke 14:21	Luke 14:12–14
Luke 14:24	Matthew 21:43; Luke 13:22–30

Things to Think About

- Do you think charity dinners are a legitimate form of charitable work, or are people who can afford to enjoy themselves simply purchasing a feel-good factor?

- Think of some good things you have done recently or in times past. Can you remember what your motivation was?

- Has your motivation for doing good changed over the years? How so?

- Do you agree that many of the poor in our economy can help themselves?

- How are we to understand the difference between people in need who *can* and who *cannot* be helped to help themselves?

- Do you think you and your friends do enough charitable work? If not, why?

- In what ways do you do charitable work? Can you list some things you could do on a regular basis and on a yearly basis?

- When a business does charitable work, do you think it is just a form of public relations—or is there a genuine commitment to the local community?

- Do you know of any businesses that do exceptional charitable work? Could your church do a study of local businesses and support them in their aims?

CHAPTER 14

How Much Do We
Need to Live On?

The Parable of the Lost Coin

LUKE 15:8–10

Introduction

This brief but important parable compares finding a lost coin to finding treasure in heaven. In our economy a penny may mean little, yet to the poor it may mean a lot. We will use this final parable to explore the difference between having great wealth and having little wealth. The response of the woman points us toward how we handle our money and what it means to us. Jesus is telling us that it should also point us beyond money to repentance.

The Parable

"Or suppose a woman has ten silver coins
and loses one. Does she not light a lamp, sweep
the house and search carefully until she finds it?
And when she finds it, she calls her friends and
neighbors together and says, 'Rejoice with me; I
have found my lost coin.' In the same way, I tell
you, there is rejoicing in the presence of the angels
of God over one sinner who repents."

The Reflection

There is an old saying in England: look after the pennies and the pounds will look after themselves. Another expression refers to going to the restroom as "spending a penny," because at one time it cost a penny to go into a public restroom. Inflation has cast extreme doubt on both of these sayings. "Looking after pennies" just won't do. I wonder how many of us would bother searching for a penny if we dropped one in a store and it rolled under the counter. We would probably leave it. As for "spending a penny," we need at least twenty of them at a railway station now, I venture.

Likewise this parable. It seems absurd that the woman should exert so much effort in search of a single silver coin and then tell her neighbors all about it. However, this silver coin was a drachma, equivalent to one day's pay. (No single coin is worth that in our economy today, except for specially minted gold and silver coins.) In the United States, the current minimum wage is $5.15 an hour, which would be equal to a coin worth $41.20 for an eight-hour day. Now that sounds like a lot more, doesn't it? Yet to a billionaire this is less than pocket change. But to someone living in poverty, $41.20 is a princely sum indeed. The fact is that the value of money depends on how much of it you already have. How much would a single coin have to be worth before you would behave as the woman does in this parable? To put it another way, how much do you need to live on—and how much can you afford to lose?

I suspect that if any of us were to subject our neighbors to this exuberant response to finding, let's say, a penny coin, they would think we obviously don't get out much. Of course to us a penny is kind of small and insignificant, like the average day's wage is to a billionaire. Perhaps we would have to win the lottery or a game show to get this excited (and we can see this on our television any night of the week). For this woman, it was indeed a lot. For those who are living in poverty today in developing countries, it would also have great value. One can well imagine people there in search of one coin since they live on less than a dollar a day. And over a billion people in the world do live on such a sum.

I wonder how we view our personal wealth. Do we assume that when we talk about the wealthy we are referring to other people—like Bill Gates or Richard Branson or Madonna or Bono? Well, these are the super rich. And as an aside we should understand that many celebrities have in fact become corporations, and the celebrities themselves are the chief executive officers. However, as we discussed in an earlier parable, all of us are comparatively wealthy, especially when we look at that figure of a dollar a day. Even for us, a penny may vary in value, depending on our financial situation. When we have difficulties and the bills are mounting up, we often say that "every penny counts." The cash in our wallets and purses that we ordinarily take for granted may become quite important when we have to scrape together enough coins and dollar bills to pay a long-overdue bill. The wealthier we get, the smaller and more insignificant a penny gets. But what counts for "watching the pennies" becomes exponential to our wealth—the end point being that when rich people fall they have a long way to drop. We've all heard stories of one-time celebrities or successful businesspeople who have hit hard times and become cabbies or store clerks or even homeless. It is all relative.

If we look beyond our own financial needs and difficulties, we can compare ourselves to others and see that perhaps we are not as bad off as we had thought. By this I mean looking at how much we need to live and how much we spend on things not necessary for a good existence. We live economically between what we need to spend to get by and what we would like to have to feel comfortable. We should ask ourselves to whom we are comparing our lot: "the Joneses" or people worse off than us? The former case is all about keeping up social appearances and getting on with improving our standing in the community. The latter case has to do with what we really need to subsist. Of course, we may feel that things are pretty much on an even keel, that we're doing pretty well and don't need to aspire to more than we have. We could also look at those who are not as well-off as we are and feel guilty that we are so favored, which seems to be a problem highlighted by poverty protests.

We can take it as a given that prophecy should direct us *toward* the ills of life, not away from them. Many of the poverty protestors see themselves standing in the prophetic tradition, directing us to the inequality and senselessness of poverty. Is this prophecy? Is there even room to question what this means? Well, if you have gotten this far in the book, you will not be surprised to read that there are questionable elements of this prophetic stance. This is not to say that there is no scope for an authentic prophetic role to be played by Christians. However, prophecy certainly means more than one-time publicity stunts that generate a feel-good factor, directing us away from the problem by helping us appease our guilt.

The problem of poverty requires, rather, more than a party and feel-good march; it requires good economics and good government. Do those who gather at such protests feel the same love or concern for their neighbors? Do they have the same worries about the poor communities close to them? Is it in fact easier to objectify the poor, lay the blame at others' doors, and demand that the government do more—and thereby direct attention away from the guilt that humanity shares in its separation from God?

In such protests, we become consumers of poverty. The music will sell. The newspapers will sell. Many will feel that they have accomplished something, although they will, I'm afraid, achieve little. The governments represented at global meetings are well aware of the poverty problems. Some are stronger advocates than others. There are many players involved in solving the problems; and of course the self-interest of all nations is a factor. When your own country has problems or you have become credit-dependent on the economy, how far are you prepared to go for the poor? How much of your mortgage will you risk?

We have a fragile economy that is being run on the fuel of our desires, of our self-interest. We have noted Adam Smith's view of self-interest in which he famously stated that it is not on the kindness of the butcher and the baker that we trade but upon our self-interest. What Smith meant is that trade is not conducted by people out of the goodness of their heart, but because they have their own needs and interests to consider first. This was how Smith stated the issue in the *Wealth of Nations*, but opponents equate this self-interest with selfishness. In *The Theory of Moral Sentiments*, Smith defines self-interest not in terms of selfishness but in terms of what is beneficial for the survival and happiness of the self. The selfish thing, the desire for what we can consume, may not be in our self-interest. The headlong rush toward debt and consumerism may owe more to our selfish desires than to our own interests.

Of course, from the parable we know that there is much more to the story than our own desires and interests. The parable of the lost coin is very much like the parable of the lost sheep that precedes it (Luke 15:3–7), but Jesus has chosen here to use an economic example. It is also similar to the parables of hidden treasure and a valuable pearl (Matthew 13:44–46). The lost coin points us toward the repentant sinner, while the treasure and pearl point us toward the kingdom of heaven. These parables reveal a different kind of economy, an economy that at once breaks apart all that we are and have materially: an economy of gift. It is no ordinary coin, but a silver coin. The coin is of great significance to the woman, as we see from her joy, but may not hold the same meaning for others—though arguably it should! It is no ordinary lost object; it is hidden treasure. It is no ordinary piece of jewelry; it is a pearl. Each parable indicates something precious and something that is gifted to the finder in some way.

The gospel is a gift given to us—something that is precious but yet costs us no money—which leads us to ask whether it thus subverts the human economy. At the risk of deconstructing capitalism, we could cite that doyen of postmodernism, Jacques Derrida, who provided a wonderful insight when he wrote that the problem of gift is that it breaks the cycle of exchange in the economy. Derrida's proposal is that the gift subverts the real objective of all economic transactions because our acts of economic transaction are all calculations. Thus gift has no place in the economy, which is perhaps why economists would call a gift an externality. However, perhaps a gift also becomes a source of doubt in the economy because gifts are ultimately more valuable and meaningful than the things we buy or covet for ourselves. The gift suggests that we act in a way that is wholly other, that we give up our self-interest as selfish. Yet, if we give, or forgive, are we not still making a calculation?

It seems that we want the economy to do that which we personally do not want to do: to serve or be charitable. We do not want to give ourselves, so we subcontract to the state. I am not suggesting here that charity will solve everything (though it would go a long way). Rather, I wonder to what extent we abdicate our responsibility to care, expecting others— government agencies, welfare, the state—to do our bidding. The price we pay is perhaps small, and we expect a big dividend from it, one that takes away our guilt. A gift also becomes indebtedness, for gifts are not truly given freely, and the gift becomes part of the cycle of exchange, for there is a symbolic debt or duty created in the act of giving. The one to whom I give becomes indebted to me. Can we ever give truly selflessly?

Derrida and other writers have taken this discussion of gift further, and in these postmodern times there is a tendency toward wishful thinking in imagining an alternative economy to the free market. This is taking a good idea in the wrong direction. Absolutely, there is tension between economic life and the life of faith. Economic life appeals to our self-interest, rewarding us for our self-interest, as well as punishing us when we manage our wealth badly. The free market system is truest to our nature, and money provides a measure of how well we as individual economic agents, businesses, other economic organizations, and governments play the game. Yet the life of faith asks us to give ourselves up, to be selfless toward our neighbor. But few, if any, of us are so capable. We are then held hostage by the economy, caught in a struggle between our economic self-maximization and our selflessness, for which we receive no economic reward.

In many ways I have been at pains in this book to defend the free market system against theological attack. However, the overall aim has been to rectify a perceived bias against the market and to argue that the market is something Christians and churches can and should work with for the better. Theology should not exclude the market, since the market is the best form of economic organization we have at our disposal at present. Within this limited framework there is much that can be achieved for the good. To this view, I add a major caveat. The market is not the place for us to find salvation, nor should we use the economy as a means to shore up our own independence from God. The values of the gospel are, in the ultimate court, contrary to the market—but this applies just as much to all else in this world that is at odds with the gospel.

The gospel shines light on all the dark recesses of human life and shows how often we fall short of the ideal. Against this gospel we are to measure all that we are and do, and act to align ourselves with the Lord in battle against evil and the wrongs of the world. This is a daily struggle, since we rise and die with Christ each day; and it is also a lifelong struggle as we seek the kingdom of God. As this parable ends, Jesus tells us that there is joy in the presence of the angels of God over one sinner who repents. The gospel calls for us all to repent, rich and poor. It is the gift we are given to guide us in all our ways and is thus outside of the economy and outside of human society. There can be no trading for this gift, there is nothing we can give to equal the generosity of the gift, and we are wholly undeserving of the gift. We can and should seek to do good in the world, but there is only one source of grace and only one appropriate response. God is that source of grace, and the appropriate response is to kneel and give thanks in the name of Jesus Christ that it is freely offered to us. There is no other way to achieve salvation.

Secular salvation—where we make our concern and care for the poor the source of our spiritual well-being (and in some cases our economic well-being as well)—is no substitute. I leave you with this unsettling image from a short story by the nineteenth-century French poet Charles Baudelaire, which Derrida discusses, where a man passes a counterfeit coin to a beggar, leaving the impression of giving a generous gift. Baudelaire writes of the response by the man's friend:

> I looked him squarely in the eyes and I was appalled to see that his eyes shone with unquestionable candour. I then saw clearly that his aim had been to do a good deed while at the same time making a good deal; to earn forty cents and the heart of God; to win paradise economically; in short, to pick up gratis the certificate of a charitable man.

Other Biblical Texts to Study

Luke 15:8   Luke 15:4, 11–16

Luke 15:9   Luke 15:5–6, 17 24

Luke 15:10   Luke 15:7, 25–32

Things to Think About

- How much money would you have to lose before you became worried? Or, alternatively, how much money would it take to make you as excited as the woman in the parable?

- How do you understand the differences between people in poverty, the average wage earner, and the really wealthy?

- How much do you really *need* to live on?

- Do you agree that many of those who protest poverty have become "consumers of poverty"?

- Is it good that celebrities raise the profile of campaigns by their involvement, or do you think they abuse their status?

- Do you agree that selfishness and self-interest are different? Is it possible to act in a positive, self-interested way?

- In what ways is the gospel a subversive gift?

- Is it true that we expect the government to appease our guilt in the economy?

- Have we become cynical about doing good deeds, about caring for those less fortunate?

CHAPTER 15

THE GOSPEL IN AN ECONOMIC
WORLD IN NEED OF FAITH

*You know, it's said that an economist is the only professional
who sees something working in practice and then seriously
wonders if it works in theory.*

—RONALD REAGAN

Two stark insights need to be kept in mind as we consider
Jesus' economic parables. The first is that they include many

more references to economic issues than is often appreciated. The second is that the disciples and the early church lived in communities, founded on generosity and almsgiving. How different the New Testament world and our economic world of today!

However, neither from the parables themselves nor from the practice of the early church can we draw any systematic biblical economic model. What we are faced with in these parables is a challenge to the way we live now—a challenge produced by Jesus' message and by the way the earliest disciples understood how they were to follow him.

The Bible sets out by telling us how God has provided for us in his creation and how we are separated from God by original sin. To help us exist in his creation, he has given us many resources and many tools—and the creative impulse to harness these resources and skillfully employ the tools at our disposal. The way in which we have organized ourselves economically has evolved in the many centuries since Adam was forced out of the garden and was told how difficult it would be to work the land.

Today we organize our resources according to capitalist market economies that involve competitive markets and pursuit of profits. Critics of this approach tend to point to corporate scandals or high bonuses awarded to company presidents as proof that the capitalist system is corrupt. However, the abuse of economic tools is not a conclusive argument against the free market system, just as much as rape does not make sex wrong.

Yet this so often seems the end of the argument for opponents of free enterprise.

Can it not be that God has given us the mechanism of the market and economics to organize our complex global population, just as he has given us science to cure disease? Such an argument is usually immediately scoffed at, but why? Robert Nozick's suggestion that it is because intellectuals resent the fact that the market economy does not recognize their worth may equally apply to theologians and church leaders. For this reason, theologians and church leaders rally against capitalism, rather than follow the biblical example evident throughout the discussion of these economic parables. Jesus was more pragmatic in his view, but then again he was a carpenter and not a Pharisee or church leader.

In the parables we have studied together, Jesus took everyday examples from nature and mundane life to explain how great and wonderful is the kingdom of God. He would start by saying something like "The kingdom of God is like . . . ," which resonates or strikes a chord in our nature because everything comes from God. Thus, we can see God at work in the economy. In a negative sense, this goes back to the beginning and the banishment of Adam: "The man has now become like one of us, knowing good and evil. He must not be allowed to reach out his hand and take also from the tree of life and eat, and live forever. So the LORD God banished him from the Garden of Eden to work the ground from which he had been taken" (Genesis 3:22–23).

Economic organization is required in our modern world for the earth to yield its sustaining goodness and for a community to be sustained by its people. To "work the ground from which we have been taken" is so much more demanding today. With a large population to sustain, the task is so much more complex than in smaller societies such as those recalled in Scripture.

Jesus' parables rely on the notion that the natural order of things is divinely ordered in some way, which may explain why he can put nature to work in the parables so vividly. The details given are not independent of the story, although they are not about specific places or the place where Jesus is teaching. They achieve significance only through the story, which the hearers understand because Jesus uses ordinary and readily recognizable elements of the rural economy or life in a small town or neighborhood. There is an affinity between natural order and the spiritual dimension that helps us to understand these words of Jesus.

This affinity with the natural order remains today, and our spiritual thirst equally needs to be quenched. We can talk about a material economy and a spiritual economy, both of which demand that we use our resources carefully. As Jesus observed, if we cannot be trusted with the little things, how can we be trusted with the big things?

Our material concerns are different than those of the hearers who first listened to Jesus talk about the economic world. Like those first hearers, we seek to survive. But today we strive to provide for our future financially through savings, pensions, and health care. From early in our lives we assume we have a long life ahead of us (but need to provide for our dependents should our lives be cut short). This is not unreasonable because most of us do live longer—a reality that is currently causing concerns in many economies as older populations need to be sustained economically.

Yet we still face the same spiritual quest as those first hearers: How are we to live? What Jesus is driving us toward is for us to answer how often we live our life "as if." We are to live as if we stand constantly judged, as if we might be taken tomorrow. Do we not, in fact, live complacently in the spiritual economy?

The parables of Jesus constantly underline the crisis of our existence. Living in the economy we can tend to think of our lives as meaningful in purely economic terms: doing our job, working for a higher pay packet, putting money into savings. This is important, but it is not everything. Ultimately, this is not a life of ledgers and adequate provision, long-term financial planning and preparation for retirement. This is about a crisis of decision, the crisis of living out our life as if our very existence is under threat. This crisis creates a call to action: not to overthrow the world order and its rulers but to recognize the rule of God in the here and now. Whatever the economic situation of humanity, his kingdom is paramount.

We are invited to listen to these parables with their depictions of ordinary life and then to make a decision on the outcome Jesus shows us. The point is made to us, as much as to the original hearers, that the time for decision is now and that this ordinary life of ours is the stage for our decision. These are no mere stories of moral generalities. Neither are these stories that are told as a part of wisdom literature or by the founder of a school of philosophy. They are dramatic portrayals of our life as it is and as it should be, rooted in our very experience so that we can understand.

What is clear from these parables is that Jesus has not proposed a radical alternative economic or political form of organization. It is an act of pure speculation to advocate such a view. Nor is Jesus seeking a perfection of human society. In him, the kingdom of God is with us; but we are in a crisis of decision about our status in the next world, not this world. All that we do in this world should flow from this decision and guide our actions. This world is the stage for a divine drama in which we play our small and humbling part.

Before Jesus there was the Law, but he set this aside and broke through the veneer of legalism and piety to demand our response. He demands our living for him and in him. There is no other place to look for salvation, no other way to gain entry to the great banquet that awaits all who accept his offer of a place at his table. Those who seek his kingdom on this earth, or fight to establish a new order based on his gospel, are acting on materialist and humanist assumptions.

The Gospels and the parables do not record a call to political and economic activism. They look outside of history, outside of our limited vision of existence. The gospel requires faith in the world to come, which is contrary to the confidence that has been fed by human thought since the Enlightenment. The gospel does not represent faith in what we can achieve but in what God can achieve in us. The Enlightenment confidence has since given way to postmodern doubt in what humanity can achieve for itself, and so our confidence is more fragile than ever. This has created a crisis in humanity. The gospel can only inspire confidence because it is not about us but about God.

Thus we live between the now and the not yet, a place of tension between our knowledge of this world and our faith in what awaits us in the next world. The history of the world is not one of economic evolution or the increase of political freedoms but a record of the continual crisis that confronts all individuals where God continually asks us what choice we will make.

There has been a long tradition, as we have noted, of Christian thinkers who have sought to imagine another world, an alternative economy. If we take the banishment of Adam seriously, then we have little option but to accept that we have the economy and world of work that we deserve. Yet the search is on for a Christian economy, and bookshelves are filled with works calling us to implement economic solutions based on a theological vision.

This is not what Jesus did in these parables. Jesus constantly calls us, but he does not coerce us into faith. The choice is ours. How then can we seek to enforce a Christian economy on others? The capitalist economy allows all of faith and no faith at all to trade and organize society freely. In these parables we see ourselves as Jesus sees us. The economic realism of his parables is part of their durability. They can hold meaning in the context of any economy the readers are subject to.

One attempt at an alternative economic view has been Christian socialism, both as a school of thought and as an implicit presence within the thought of many church groups and individuals. This approach is to be excluded from any economic interpretation of the parables as a contradiction in terms. Socialism is based on a confidence in what humanity can achieve for itself; and even when it eschews utopias, socialism still heads in that general direction. In a fallen world a utopia is not possible. Socialism is immediately at odds with a fallen world.

What about others who would propose a better economic world? Once we look a little beneath the surface of such positions, we find the same view of humanity at work: the latent wish fulfillment of socialist economics. There is a limit to the extent of planning and social engineering that can be successful, which is why socialism ultimately fails. And it is planning and social engineering that lies at the heart of many arguments that imagine a better economic world.

Are we then to be otherworldly? Are we to see Christianity as a spiritual faith alone? The parables we have studied suggest emphatically not, just as they do not support social economic planning or social engineering. The parables are able to point clearly to our responsibilities and to what stands between us and God. They do not provide any policy options on how we can carry out our responsibilities, however, nor do they offer a vision of a better world. This leaves us with a tension. We have responsibilities in this world, and we have the world we inherited from Adam.

The study of the economic world since Adam is a fascinating one, and there is not room in this book to examine this history. The situation today is that we can see that what historically seems to work is capitalism. The worry we all have is that our economy allows many elements that Christians need to reject—such as violence, greed, pornography, and any number of concerns—to flourish. Again, these concerns have a history longer than that of capitalism.

Since the early days of capitalism, there has been reaction against it. The single most organized reaction to capitalism has been communism. The destructiveness of communism as an alternative to free enterprise has to be seen for what it was. Yet, although it denied economic benefits and freedoms, communism played a role for all the decades of its existence as a foil for Christians and intellectuals who wanted to pretend there is an alternative for us to dream, even though *that* alternative did not work. Little attention was given by intellectuals to the economic and human failings of communism because it served as a useful contrast to attack capitalism, as movement after movement denounced capitalism and its competitive instincts.

Has the competitive element of capitalism really caused the same level of suffering as communism? Despite the failure, on a massive scale, of a planned economy, there is still an insistence that a competitive market is inherently sinful and cannot possibly solve the problems of the world. Who should this task be left to? Why, the government—meaning the politicians and civil servants—of course. If we look at the most recent emerging capitalist economy of China, what sector is growing the most? The public sector.

If we ignore the solution of large economic programs, how are we then to counter the objections to specific elements of the market economy? The elements of profit, private property, and selfish acquisition are proffered as self-evident objections that militate against a positive view of the capitalist economy. So let us look at these elements more closely.

Profit tops the list of things in the market that are attacked. In such attacks it seems as if profit is to be morally distanced because it is seen as inherently sinful. The case is made that profit dominates us and distorts behavior. This is wholly at odds with the view of Jesus, who constantly warned us about ourselves, not some imagined sinful structure of society. In the parable of the talents, it is the one who makes good use of his capital who is singled out for praise.

The attack on profit suggests a world dominated by people in big business who are evil profit-mongers. In an imagined alternative economy, they could be saved and become good community-spirited folk. This is a false appraisal of the economic world. There are many well-intentioned businesspeople who want business success that creates many good outcomes. Companies and entrepreneurs typicially want to employ a happy workforce and be a positive presence in their community. Besides all this, the lust for profit by no means assures its achievement, for many businesses fail in such pursuit.

Another objection is one made about private property—by people who have private property themselves, one might add. Over the years I have met many a socialist with a better zip code than mine or who owned property while I rented. The capitalist economy is built on the exchange between private owners of goods and capital, and it does not distinguish between their political views. In capitalism, socialists can live well without anyone telling them what to do with their property. In socialism, capitalists are denied freedom in ownership by imposition of taxes and regulations that seek to socially engineer. In his economic parables, Jesus assumed private ownership, not questioning private ownership in itself but the way in which the owner behaved.

Another line of attack is that the market promotes selfishness. In earlier chapters we have had cause to refer to self-interest as the catalyst of wealth creation, and we have challenged the automatic assumption that equates self-interest with selfishness. When we love God, then we act in the self-interest of that love, or what the twelfth-century monastic writer Bernard of Clairvaux called the "love of self for God's sake." Such self-interest, which also suggests self-love, spurns selfishness as destructive of the love of self for God's sake. There are many times when the selfish thing to do can be destructive of one's self-interest. The economic world, which is based on the real world as it is rather than as we would wish it to be, is based on recognizing this self-interest as the mechanism for making the market work.

Competition is another area that frequently concerns critics of the market. Yet we can say that competition is simply mediation. It is a way of resolving conflicting wants in society, and it permits freedom of choice of products and services. You can choose to buy a book condemning the market—or one supporting it. You can buy expensive organic food—or you can buy cheaper food and donate the difference to charity. The choice is yours. The suppliers of both McDonald's hamburgers and organic farmers compete for your dollars. Bono and African charities both compete for your dollars as well. In making a choice we consider cost, which is made up of what an item costs the supplier and how much profit can be had. The alternative is to set prices artificially, but we are then left to ponder who should set them and how.

Finally, though not exhaustively, there is the charge that the market promotes inequality. The parables we have studied assume people have different economic statuses. It is indeed a fact that the market allows for inequality, but then again, what society has ever been truly egalitarian? Inequality is not an inherent quality of the economy but a fact of life in all economies. The market rewards wants and reconciles scarcity. It does not attach value to the moral demand of any particular person or class of persons. Therefore, a nurse is paid less than a rock star because people have greater wants for music than health care. Water is plentiful in most places and is free or charged at a low price, whereas diamonds are scarce.

The Christian attacks on the market have historically been holistic in nature, in that the system of capitalism is seen as lacking legitimacy. The failure of communism, and the lack of any alternative successful model to replace it, has weakened the attack of late, leading to reluctant acceptance of elements of the market economy. This is a grudging acceptance inspired by the failure of alternatives rather than a recognition of the success of the market economy model. The argument tends to fall back on the specific criticisms we have just examined. In short, there appears to be what we referred to in earlier chapters: a fundamental animus against the market.

The point that this book seeks to make is that the market system is not contrary to Christianity, and its alternatives are not morally superior either—quite the reverse by all historical accounts. However, this is not to say that the market is necessarily of divine provision, though that is definitely a debate worth having, as suggested by parallels with other mechanisms in human life. By selecting these various parables, the aim has been to suggest points of reflection on the market economy that govern much of our day-to-day life and explore points of comparison with the way in which Jesus talked about economic matters. A final aim has been to expose some of the assumptions that Christians make about economic matters and to challenge the theological validity of these assumptions. When looked at closely, the conclusion is ventured that many Christian objections are really political arguments given a religious veneer.

A happy outcome (hopefully) of our study is that Christians can argue about policy solutions with political assumptions isolated as to what is pragmatically possible (and politics is famously the art of the possible), but with a shared understanding of what the Bible is telling them. The likely result is that we can all share the biblical concerns over poverty, inequality, greed, and other issues while disagreeing about the policy options that can lead to the best outcome. What is ruled out is any notion that there is a Christian economic solution to the problems for all the complex reasons that we have explored together in these economic parables. I hope that through studying these parables Christians can hear what Jesus really intended them to be: stories about ourselves, a fallen people trying to get by, in the hope that—whatever our economic status—we will find our way home to him.

This is not to say that economics is completely morally neutral because it involves making decisions, and all human decisions involve moral choices. The aim is to extricate economics from the grasp of theologians and church people who would Christianize economic policy, one way or another. The economy is more akin to a knife, as we have observed, which can be used to cut bread or wound a fellow human being—used for good or bad. Capitalism is the sharpest knife we have in our grasp; it has pulled millions out of poverty in the last century and will continue to do so in this one. Any view that tries to marry theology to radical economics is doomed to failure because it is getting the issues the wrong way around. The task undertaken here by looking at the parables has been to reverse this flow, to clarify how we can think theologically about the economic world in which we live, and to consider how we can take the gospel to an economic world in need of faith.

RESOURCES FOR
FURTHER STUDY

Books written from a
theological perspective:

Atherton, John. *Christianity and the Market.* London: SPCK, 1992.

Bonhoeffer, Dietrich. *Dietrich Bonhoeffer Works, Volume 4: Discipleship.* Edited by Geffrey B. Kelly and John D. Godsey. Translated by Martin Kuske and Ilse Todt. Minneapolis: Augsburg Fortress, 2001.

Bulgakov, Sergii. *Towards a Russian Political Theology.* Edited by Rowan Williams. Edinburgh: T & T Clark, 1999.

Childs, James M. Jr. *Ethics in Business: Faith at Work.* Minneapolis: Fortress Press, 1995.

——. *Greed: Economics and Ethics in Conflict.* Minneapolis: Fortress Press, 2000.

Dodd, C. H. *Parables of the Kingdom.* New York: Scribner, 1961.

Ellul, Jacques. *The Ethics of Freedom.* Oxford: Mowbrays, 1976.

Forrester, Duncan B. *Christian Justice and Public Policy.* Cambridge: Cambridge University Press, 1997.

Gorringe, Timothy J. *Capital and the Kingdom.* New York: Orbis/SPCK, 1994.

Griffiths, Brian. *The Creation of Wealth.* London: Hodder and Stoughton, 1984.

Hay, Donald. *Economics Today: A Christian Critique.* Leicester, UK: Apollos, 1989.

Jeremias, Joachim. *The Parables of Jesus.* London: SCM Press, 1972.

Krueger, David A., Donald W. Shriver Jr, and Laura L. Nash. *The Business Corporation and Productive Justice.* Nashville: Abingdon, 1997.

Long, Stephen D. *Divine Economy: Theology and the Market.* London: Routledge, 2000.

Meeks, Douglas M. *God the Economist.* Minneapolis: Fortress Press, 1989.

Norman, Edward. *Entering the Darkness: Christianity and Its Modern Substitutes.* London: SPCK, 1991.

Novak, Michael. *The Catholic Ethic and the Spirit of Capitalism.* New York: Free Press, 1993.

Preston, Ronald H. *Religion and the Ambiguities of Capitalism.* London: SCM Press, 1991.

Taylor, Michael. *Poverty and Christianity.* London: SCM Press, 2000.

Books written from an economic or social perspective:

Bhagwati, Jagdish. *In Defense of Globalization.* New York: Oxford University Press, 2004.

Derrida, Jacques. *Given Time: 1. Counterfeit Money.* Translated by Peggy Kamuf. Chicago: University of Chicago Press, 1992.

Easterley, William. *The White Man's Burden: Why the West's Efforts to Aid the Rest Have Done So Much Ill and So Little Good.* New York: Penguin, 2006.

Friedman, Milton. *Capitalism and Freedom.* Chicago: University of Chicago Press, 1982.

Friedman, Thomas L. *The Lexus and the Olive Tree: Understanding Globalization.* New York: Anchor Books, 2000.

Fukuyama, Francis. *Trust: The Social Virtues and the Creation of Prosperity.* New York: Free Press, 1995.

Giddens, Anthony. *The Third Way and Its Critics.* Cambridge, UK: Polity Press, 2000.

Gray, John. *False Dawn.* London: Granta Books, 1998.

Hayek, F. A. *The Mirage of Social Justice, Volume 3: Law, Legislation and Liberty.* London: Routledge, 1998.

Marx, Karl. *Grundrisse: Foundations of the Critique of Political Economy.* Translated by Martin Nicolaus. London: Penguin, 1993.

Nozick, Robert. *Anarchy, State, and Utopia.* New York: Basic Books, 1977.

————. *Socratic Puzzles.* Boston: Harvard University Press, 1999.

Roll, Eric. *A History of Economic Thought.* London: Faber and Faber, 1992.

Sachs, Jeffrey. *The End of Poverty: Economic Possibilities for Our Time.* New York: Penguin, 2006.

Sen, Amartya. *Development as Freedom.* New York: Anchor Books, 1999.

Stiglitz, Joseph E. *Globalization and Its Discontents.* New York: Norton, 2003.

Smith, Adam. *The Theory of Moral Sentiments.* Indianapolis: Liberty Classics, 1976.

————. *The Wealth of Nations.* New York: Everyman's Library, 1991.

Tawney, R. H. *Religion and the Rise of Capitalism: A Historical Study.* London: John Murray, 1944.

Weber, Max. *The Protestant Work Ethic and the Spirit of Capitalism.* London: Routledge, 2000.

Wolf, Martin. *Why Globalization Works.* New Haven, CT: Yale University Press, 2004.

AFTERWORD

The events of Fall 2008 call for special attention in this second edition, and there are many observations to make that suit the specific events of that turbulent period, and serve as warning signs for what lies ahead of us economically.

While the media pondered if this was the end of capitalism, and European politicians looked at American capitalism with a smirk of self-satisfaction, it seemed only a matter of time before we could look for the movie The Last Days of the Capitalist Empire. If only there were someone left to finance the production. However, we should not be so hasty. Capitalism is not about to end, so bang goes that storyline.

The real story is what the sequel for capitalism will be. Its doom has been predicted from the moment Adam Smith played midwife to the economic science of capitalism. The thing to remember is that Smith was a moral philosopher, and we have been morally troubled ever since. The animus towards capitalism has stalked it across the continents; with intellectual opposition rising every time there is a problem. This is always accompanied by a moral yearning for a more secure economic world.

What we learn from Adam's (not Smith but the biblical one) banishment from the Garden of Eden is that working with scarce resources was never going to be easy. Chapter 3 verse 23 reads "So the Lord God banished him from the Garden of Eden to work the ground from which he had been taken", and after he was driven out, he was placed on the east side of the Garden of Eden. We are well and truly on the east side of the economic Garden of Eden we thought we were living in these past decades.

For past decades we have behaved like spoiled children, and now that the fun is over we are stamping our feet demanding to know who is responsible. Well, we all are. The current crisis has to be put into perspective. As a spoiled society, we have become only happy in the good times and unprepared for the bad times. Unlike our parents and grandparents, we forgot to save for a rainy day and thought only of things getting better. This was unrealistic.

Recent events have demonstrated once more that the economy has its own rules of gravity, what goes up will come down. We didn't hear complaints when it was easy to get loans, without backing it up with any assets, but now that the markets have gone against us we don't want to take responsibility. The financial industry has to take risks, and when they get it right no one complains, but when they get it wrong, then out comes the age-old animus towards capitalism; if only the economic behaviour of individuals were so predictable!

So, this is not the time to question the future of capitalism. It is not a question of whether capitalism works or not. It is not a time to go back to the tired old debates of the last century about capitalism. The alternatives like socialism and communism caused oppression, and they were unsuccessful. We still believe in democracy, even when elected leaders have become dictators. Equally, we still have to believe in capitalism, even when we see irresponsible leadership in the market.

This is the question to ask: what kind of capitalism do we want? The answer should not be a kind of European socialist-lite. It should be robust capitalism, made robust by effective regulation, increased individual responsibility by all, and greater accountability of financial institutions and businesses so that managers actually know what is going on in their organizations.

It is in this economic context that Christians have to tackle the questions posed in the economic parables. We can start by asking, how have we prepared for this? This means questioning our own role. We can't just point at Wall Street or government and blame them. We are part of the market. It is inter-connected. Our demand drives this. If we think that bankers are greedy, fine, but let's look at our own greed as well.

What happened in Fall 2008 is a bleak message to us all; we know that. But there is a bleaker message when we do not listen to Jesus when he tells the rich man in the parable "You can't take it with you." If you are hurting right now from this economic crisis, you have to ask yourself what you have left, and you should see indeed there is much left, for there is the love of Jesus in your life. Just like the economy, this is an opportunity for you show him that you can go through the bad times with him, not just the good times.

Many people, as they find their material life difficult, will also find they have nothing left in the spiritual bank, because they have based their life on material things. If we base our life on the parables, we learn that Jesus tells us to use our worldly wealth wisely, so this is a time to ask, did we do that? Did we do that economically? And more importantly, did we do that spiritually?

For the faithful who have managed both their economical and spiritual wealth wisely, this is a time for you to reach out into your community and see how you can help people in trouble. Help people with debt counselling, and give people spiritual counselling. When 9/11 and New Orleans happened we knew we had to reach out. This is an economic storm we are in, and we need the same approach; money doesn't make it different.

What we really need is a change of attitude towards the way we are living our lives, and that also means a change of heart. This is a time for Christians to remind ourselves and our neighbors that a lifestyle change does not depend on the economy, but prepares us better for dealing with economic problems. This means turning to Christ, and suddenly we will find our priorities changing and we will become less dependent upon material things. To show true discipleship in bad economic times does not need money. It needs prayerful attention to our own problems and active support for our neighbor who may be worse off than we are. Our time and support may be just what our neighbor needs right now!

To go back to the opening point, the sequel to Fall 2008 will no doubt be increased responsibility . . . until the next time? However, there is an opportunity to fix this. Capitalism is very good at measuring what we are, and as the last chapter of the book states, it is like a mirror which reflects what our society wants. This means there is an even greater opportunity to look in the mirror and be honest, and ask ourselves, Do we like what we see? At the moment we look and see a reflection like someone who has only managed two hours sleep after an all night party. The last thing we need is the make-up artists to come in and make like we're pretty again.